Yogini's Guide
Intuition Is A Choice

Candace McKim
Illustrated by Chloe McKim

Yogini Sarah

Follow your intuition
on every step as you live
a full and joyful life.

Love Candace

Aug 2015

"Candace is a real shining Yogini. Because she lives the union of the mind, body, spirit, she was inspired to write this beautiful book Intuition is a choice.

Yes Intuition is a choice. And intuition is not only a choice it's the only way to bring world peace. Only when the men and women will be able to follow their inner voice that is guiding them within themselves, the world will be a better place to live. Only when men and women will allow their soul to sing, there will be joy on Earth.

In a genius way, through 54 different yoga aspects, Candace's book guides you to your intuitive voice, from inner peace to outer peace."

~Amandine Roche, UN peace keeper,
yoga teacher and founder of Amanuddin Foundation

"Personal, profound and practical. Candace artfully weaves her own journey with yogic wisdom and daily practices that will enrich your life."

~Wendy E. Shumway, M.D.

"Written by a Yogini for Yogini's, Candace's book is a rare gem that weaves together the asanas, emotions, real life circumstances, and how they manifest in our physical and emotional bodies. "Yogini's Guide Intuition Is A Choice" empowers the reader to connect to the divine feminine intuition that exists for all women, with playfulness, humility and practicality."

~Nadine Wolff, Karmic Jewels
By Nadine and Co-founder of One Love, Long Island

"When you find a teacher, who is sincerely living what she teaches, who knows not only how to move our bodies, but understands the soul, the chakras and how to balance them–pay attention."

This is Candace:

"A sincere teacher whose life reflects yoga at every level. What a catch, to have found an authentic example of a teacher/healer/ practitioner. Lucky us to have found Candace, her true understanding of the ancient yogic path with a modern twist. She has it all."

~Debra Silverman,
Psychotherapist and Astrologer to the Stars

"Yogini's Guide – Intuition Is A Choice offers you new tools, practices and wisdom to connect to who you truly are as a divine intuitive human being who has the *choice* to cultivate a life of creative expression, inner peace and joy in every breath. Candace graciously shares her personal journey and how the principles of Yoga guide her to a purpose-full, harmonious and vibrant life. This book will surely transform your life in ways you never thought possible. All things are possible when we *choose* to be curious about the mystery of life and listen to the wise inner being within!"

~Karen Petersen Sainas,
Vancouver Canada

Yogini's Guide - Intuition Is A Choice

Candace McKim

Yogini's Guide Books are available for order through Ingram Press
Catalogues

Candace McKim
Visit my website at www.candacemckim.com

Printed in the United States of America
First Printing: July 2015
Published by Sojourn Publishing, LLC

ISBN: 978-1-62747-120-6

CONTENTS

Part 1
Introduction

Part 2
Asana Yoga Postures

Part 3
Chakras Energy Centers

Part 4
Aspects of Yoga Eight Limbs of Yoga

Part 5

Conclusion

Part 1

INTRODUCTION

What is YOGINI?

*Y*ogini is a woman who lives yoga. **Yoga** means to yoke together our **body** and **mind** with our **spirit**. Therefore, a Yogini may or may not go to a yoga class, yet she intends each day to move her **body** in some form, eat as healthfully as possible and does her best for physical wellness. She expands her self-awareness, stays curious and open to learning new things for her **mind**. Lastly, a Yogini connects to her soul through breathing, laughing and striving to meditate for her **spirit**. You are **Yogini**.

Yogini is a woman who tries to be everything to everyone, hoping her life appears from the outside as beautifully perfect. On the inside this woman feels something is missing, she yearns for a spiritual connection, to follow the sound of her intuition by stepping fully into her purpose and her femininity. As she continues to seek, learn and search, she experiences fear of walking wholly on that path due to ridicule, confrontation or loss of security.

Welcome to My Readers

Welcome to *Yogini's Guide-Intuition Is A Choice*. Both the deck of fifty-four cards and the book are to gain clarity with specific issues, find answers to questions, as well as insight with everyday challenges. They are great for continuing to do deep internal work, which allows us to feel the connection to our soul and the sound of our intuition. When we do regular soul searching we persist moving forward with purpose, holding our fear and ego at bay.

To begin, I have chosen fifty-four cards; this number is half of the sacred and blessed number 108. The number 108 is considered holy in many traditions including Hinduism and Yoga. There are 108 beads on a mala string used for meditation and prayer (plus an extra bead called the "guru bead"). It is also connected with the sun, moon, and earth with the average distance from the Sun and the Moon to the Earth being 108 times their diameters. As well, there are 108 sacred points or chakras in our body and we can offer the universe a blessing of performing 108 Sun Salutations at the changing of each season on the Solstices and Equinoxes.

I felt a desire to connect with spirit and get answers from my intuition for as long as I can remember. I used necklaces or a needle and thread for divination before I got my first pendulum twenty-five years ago. I purchased my first deck of oracle cards when my children were babies. I had been doing divination already for many years by that time but the cards were new, exciting and easy to use. They have since become a part of my decision making as well as keeping me motivated and listening to my intuition.

Through my lifetime of living, practicing and teaching yoga with a daily meditation practice since I was thirteen, I began to notice that when I did certain yoga postures I would get clear insight, I felt specific emotions and I would behave in a particular way. I noticed similar and related messages appearing to me during my asana (yoga postures) practice through pranayama (breath work) as well during meditation. I began to take note of this intuition and then meditated on what the messages were and how the knowledge could be beneficial.

Finally I got the clear intuition to take note and create these oracle cards and book.

I keep a knowing deep in my core, in my soul, and definitely in my heart that there is a greater energy out there that is supporting me. A force that is keeping me safe, protected, and loved; completely and unconditionally. You have your own understanding and connection to Spirit, The Divine, Universal Power, God, Goddess, Mother Earth, Truth, Source, Greater Energy, or Higher Power. Whatever you call it, I honor your own understanding and guidance. This energetic force is here for you to fully feel its presence and connect with. Communicate your desires, feel confidence like you've never experienced before and strength that will take you to do all the amazing, fierce and wonderful things you were meant to do in this lifetime. I believe that when we feel freedom in our soul, connection with unconditional love and allow ourselves to be authentic, we will all soar.

Yogini's Guide to Intuition **Oracle Cards** offer a brief description of insight to share from specific postures or aspects of yoga. *Yogini's Guide-Intuition Is A Choice* adds more wisdom and personal experiences of how I use my own spiritual guidance. I offer you tools from yoga traditions and philosophy to move through fear and discomfort into your best life possible. I yearn to always be my authentic self and to courageously value my feminine guidance. My desire is that this book will encourage you to hear the voice of your soul so that you can sing to your own unique and authentic song.

This book is a gathering from years of teaching and studying yoga, my background as a Social Worker and working in the helping field. I acknowledge all the many teachers and mentors who I have worked with or read their books. This work is in no way supporting or disregarding that you listen to your own intuition. Some of my many teachers are listed at the back of this book.

How To Do It

*T*his book was written with the intention for you to return to it whenever you want to reconnect with your intuition for clarity of a concern. To get the best results first fully read the book through.

Once you have read the book, at anytime open to a page for instant awareness, answers or inspiration. You can also use the book for one, three or five inquiry layouts, just as you would with the deck of *Yogini's Guide to Intuition Oracle Cards.*

~Hold the book in your hand and knock on the cover; this will get out any unwanted energy.

~Rub your palms together quickly and swiftly to increase your own energy.

~While holding the book in your hands ask a question, say an intention or get clear about what you want insight on.

~Ask out loud or in your mind: "Spirit, show me what I need to know."

~Flip through the book until you know when to stop. Read that chapter for insight.

For E-book use, state your inquiry and then choose a number between one and fifty-four. Read that chapter for guidance.

Layouts

One-card Layout – Instant Insight

Randomly choose one card for a quick reading. This is great to do on a daily basis for instant insight. Take a breath, mentally ask a question and then pull your card.

Three-card Layout – Body, Mind, and Spirit

Begin by taking a deep, relaxing breath. Set an intention or ask a question. The first card represents your BODY and physical health. The second card represents your MIND and emotions. Third card is your connection to and messages from SPIRIT.

Five-card Layout – Specific Situation

The first card represents your Question, the second card is for your Expectations, the third card is for Hidden Influences, with the fourth card for Advice, and the last card as your Final Outcome.

- If at anytime you feel you need to draw extra cards go ahead.
- Pay special attention to any cards that "jump" out at you.
- When cards appear upside down, check in with your intuition to identify if you are deficient or excessive in this life area.

Dedication

I dedicate this book to all the extraordinary Yogini's, Goddesses and Diva's in my life who strive to create balance and harmony, while following their souls calling. Thank you to each woman who has been hugely supportive, encouraging, and loving. You have helped guide, inspire and hold me in every stage; Mother, Sister, Daughter, Niece, Teacher, Mentor and Friend. I love and honor the unique light that is in each of you.

~Namaste

Part 2

Asana
Yoga Postures

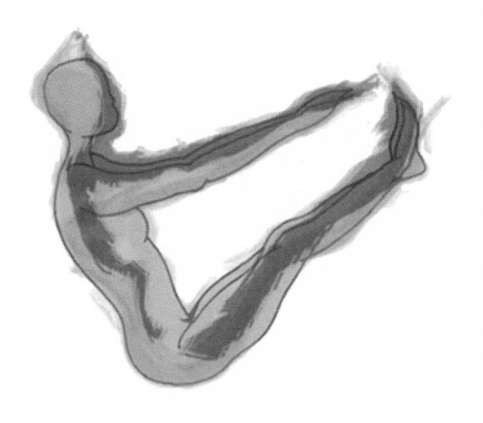

1

NAVASANA - Boat

Humor, Laughter

*N*avasana can be an extremely challenging posture that requires a lot of core strength to maintain fully. The beauty about "boat pose" is there are many levels of this posture that you can play around with. As you enter into boat, hold onto the back of your thighs, then let go, find yourself go past the discomfort, feel your excitement increase until you start to smile, chuckle, and re-grip your thighs. How do you cope? Can you see silliness in your life? Sometimes we take life too seriously and must find some humor in a situation. At times we need to be able to laugh at ourselves and how we are creating tension. Circumstances can make us angry, frustrated or fearful, but choose to make light of it; joy and laughter are strong healing elements. See if you can increase your laugh quota and add more pleasure into your life. When something is humorous really allow yourself to laugh out loud. Plan an evening with good friends that are lighthearted or bring out twister. Have some fun!

How to do it: Sitting upright on your mat, knees bent with feet flat on the mat. Hold onto the back of your thighs, slightly lean back (you will be sitting between the sit bones and the tail bone) lift feet off of the floor. When you're ready you can release your hands, straighten your legs and expand your chest. Make sure your lower belly is pulled in to protect your lower back.

*H*ow can we add more fun into our lives? Music and singing helps hugely to raise a person's vibration, change an overall mood, and to make activities more fun. As much as I enjoy solitude and quiet, I also love to add music to lift me and put me in a happier state; I dance around the kitchen and shake off a grumpy mood. Music helps tremendously with chores and with accomplishing mundane activities.

I believe strongly in girl power and spending time with girlfriends. It is particularly important to spend time with your women friends without children or a lot of responsibility for a chance to laugh and be loud, talk dirty and complain. It's fun when we can let our hair down and remember what we used to be like when we weren't working so many hours, busy with partners, pets and children. I have read that an evening with girlfriends is more beneficial than a one-hour yoga class and you know what? I think that is true. It is important to laugh out loud with friends.

When I take a look at the times in my life that have had the most fun, I am usually on an adventure, spending time with family, or having a good long chat with my girlfriends. Stay out of petty girlfriend issues and cherish the incredible women in your life.

When my children were little and our household was extremely busy I often found myself going into the bathroom for some quiet time and some space; maybe take a bath, shower or just to take a few deep breaths. It was a chance to be alone and I have always gone into the bathroom to cry and to let out my emotions. I have never been at ease with crying in front of other people and I don't like myself after I have anger outbursts, so instead I tend to head to the bathroom. In the house I grew up in we could run into the bathroom, lock the door, and then pull a drawer across the door to keep people out. It was a trick that I remember using a lot, sometimes for privacy and sometimes for protection after angering my older sister. Haha!

When my oldest two children were two and four years old, Daren and I were packing up my home that I had shared with my first husband and moving to a different city. We weren't married yet and I was taking a big risk to leave my family, lifelong friends, my business, and my home. Somehow, I just knew that it was the right decision for me to make and I've never regretted it. However, on moving day, I was beyond stressed. It was a busy day and we were packing, moving, cleaning, and sorting. I'm not sure how we were able to get it all done and organized. During the day's events and because of the stress, my stomach was doing flips and flops, I couldn't catch my breath and I felt like crying. I was anxious and I was emotional about moving away. As a result I would head to the bathroom to get myself grounded and try to bring myself back to center. EVERY single time I would be in the bathroom I could hear people calling out "Where did Candace go? What does she want done with this?" It got to the point that I had two choices. I could either laugh or cry and on that day I just laughed. I was in there for the fourth time that morning and I heard the standard "Where is Candace?" I started to laugh out loud. "I'm here." It released some of the uncertainty and nerves and I was able to be more productive to make decisions.

2

USTRASANA - Camel

Forgiveness, Acceptance

U strasana pose is about opening ourselves up to acceptance, love, and forgiveness. Just as the camel carries us across the barren dessert to the life-giving oasis, our past life history has carried us to where we are right now. Is there someone or a circumstance in your life that you can, for just this moment, entertain the idea of forgiving? Forgiveness is one of the most powerful things that we can do for our soul. Forgiveness is a gift for you when you release resentment, anger and hatred. See if you can look at the situation, detach emotionally, and shift your perception. For your own peace of mind choose to live openly to receive and accept the experiences in your life.

How to do it: Kneel on your mat, shins on the floor - hip width apart. Extend your arms up, imagine your heart center drawn up to the sky and bring your palms onto your lower back. If this is enough stay here and breathe. If available, lower your hands onto your heels. Only go as far as your body allows.

F orgiveness is one of those elusive and powerful emotions that we
know we are suppose to do, we work hard on forgiving, with the
reality that it can be extremely challenging. Remember that when
forgiving someone it does not mean that you condone how he or she
behaved. Forgiveness is to start healing and to consider that for some
reason this situation or person may be leading you in a new direction.
Acceptance means you are entertaining the idea that the experience
will lead you to a greater purpose and perhaps at this time you do not
know what it is. Forgiveness is about feeling better about the whole
circumstance, releasing hurt, blame, resentment and anger.

When you can talk about the person or hurt and it no longer has a
physical reaction in your body, you have forgiven. You can talk about
it and you have a semblance of detachment. Your stomach doesn't go
into knots, your fists don't start clenching, and your jaw doesn't
harden. You no longer feel a need to relive the story; you can speak
about it with insight and understanding. These are signs that you have
accepted, that you are not a victim or weak. In fact it takes a lot of
courage and strength of character to forgive.

My first marriage taught me how to forgive in a way that I never
thought possible. It left me with an understanding of what forgiveness
feels like, how it works and the huge benefits. Not ever having many
people to forgive, this experience allowed me to fully embody the
lesson.

When I look at that marriage, I know it was exactly what I needed
to create for myself. I learned so much about myself, as well as what I
wanted to build in a marriage. I learnt that marriage was more about
respect and acceptance than anything else, that love is expanded
through experiences. I gained knowledge that it is essential for us to
live from an authentic place.

One lesson of living my truth came very clearly; I began to
acknowledge when I was being genuine and when I was bullshitting. I

18

began to realize that I was restricting my throat chakra and how it made me feel to exaggerate.

It was a day like any other with the exception that on this day I ran into my best friend's mom. My friend and I had been buddies since we were three years old and I stopped to chat with her mom. Married to my first husband at the time, I found myself telling her something about him that wasn't true. I was embellishing a situation to make him look better, after leaving the encounter I felt horrible. This woman was someone whom I loved, honored and completely respected; yet I was lying to her. When walking away I was questioning myself and wondered why was I doing that? Why was I bullshitting her? As soon as I asked myself that question the answer popped into my head. No respect! I did not have a level of love and respect for this man and I didn't want her to know the truth. My friend's mom, as loving as ever, just listened with acceptance. But, I knew that she knew that I was exaggerating his greatness. After some time in reflection and asking: "What is it about him that isn't good enough? What was making me want to pretend that he was better, more than what he was?" That was when I realized that I didn't fully respect him. I thought I loved him but there wasn't a lot of trust or respect. I didn't think he was doing enough or was enough! He was a reflection of me, and I felt the same about myself. I didn't feel like I was doing enough or was enough. I didn't love and respect myself fully and completely either.

I would like to say that, that was it; with all this insight and realization, I was evolved enough to end the marriage. I did not. My own ego did not want me to be a failure so I stayed for several more years until our two children were born.

I lived a life where I was not completely authentic. I lived where I kept trying and trying to be someone I wasn't and to create something that wasn't there or full of value. It was many years later when the marriage ended, when it could no longer be endured and when our contract was complete.

Days after I found out I was pregnant with Chloe our relationship went from bad to even worse. By the time Chloe was born situations had escalated to violence in the hospital and when I got home. Only three months after this beautiful, gentle baby soul arrived, and we were celebrating Forrester's third birthday our marriage ended. We both knew without any doubt that our spiritual contract had concluded. We had learned the lessons that we needed to and it was time for us to no longer be together.

I went through a period of grief, and then anger and a lot of illness, but forgiveness came relatively easy for me and I think for both of us. Single parenthood was a huge challenge for me with many struggles and worries, which created more anger and resentment. We are not like some Hollywood couples where they all hang out, but honestly I feel we both quickly came to acceptance. It was not long before I could wish him well, I am happy with his successes and I don't feel any animosity towards him. We both remarried a few years later and remain in those lengthy relationships (to date I have been married to Daren for nineteen years). Forrester, Chloe and their little brother Jenkins have all become amazing adults and continue to be loved by so many people, as they are truly blessed.

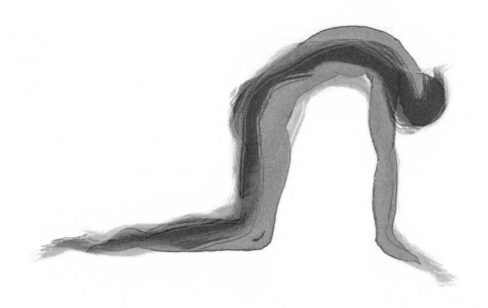

3

MARJARIASANA - Cat/Cow

Trust, Surrender

*M*arjariasana is a posture where you arch the spine one way and then the other. In Cat and Cow relax and surrender into the hopefulness of this spinal movement. Trust in yourself, your abilities, and your angels. Have faith that you will make the right phone call, you will return the precise email or meet the correct person. Prevent micro managing situations by believing in your intuition. When we try to control our life we create limitations, and increase our anxiety over the outcome. Don't drive yourself crazy with a pro and con list; have confidence you will make the right decision for you, because all your decisions will be right for you. Check in with your body and notice if you are getting a gut reaction, if the rhythm of your breathing has changed or you have an inner knowing. What is the worst that can happen if you surrender, relax and go with the flow? When we release and allow the situation to unfold organically it will create a beautiful fulfilling ease.

How to do it: Start on your hands and knees in a "tabletop" position. Make sure your knees are directly below your hips with your wrists, elbows and shoulders all stacked. Keep your head in a neutral position. Inhale lifting your tailbone up, arching the spine, allow your belly to sink down, extending shoulders and gaze up. As you exhale, round your back, pull your belly in and tuck your tailbone under. Continue to flow from cow to cat.

*F*or many of us surrendering and trusting that a situation will unfold how it is meant to be, is not an easy thing to do. We come at our decisions from many different angles and we create pro and con lists. We talk to friends and family members over and over again, hoping to make the perfect decision. Unfortunately, there is no guarantee that everything will be flawless and that we won't have to go through challenges. The fear of humiliation, looking like a fool and feeling shame is very real. Often times we put our decisions into other people's hands, even blaming them if the outcome isn't as great as we think it could have been. I know it isn't always easy to know which road to take or what choice to make and we may find ourselves in lifelong patterns of inability to make decisions.

I was spending a summer in Dawson City, Yukon in a hamlet in Northern Canada. I took my time and several weeks to travel there on my own with only a backpack, a small tent and sleeping bag. My journey began when I took a ferry from the Northern part of Vancouver Island, Port Hardy all the way to Skagway, Alaska and took the train to Whitehorse, Yukon. During the day I watched the ocean for whales and the shoreline for bald-headed eagles, at night I slept on the deck.

I stayed with a friend for a few days and then moved on to Dawson City, Yukon. That is where I set up my wee little tent in the campsite and made it my home for a couple of months. I spent my days hiking, wandering through the town, meditating and writing. I met a few friends, but this specific experience happened before I had become good friends with anyone.

I was wandering into town one morning. It was such a peaceful and beautiful environment with a campsite located across the river from the town. To access the campsite we took a riverboat and crossed the Yukon River. On one beautiful, sunny morning, I boarded the ferry to cross the river to town. When I got off the riverboat I walked the gravel road up a hill towards Dawson. Out of nowhere I realized there was a young man who was following me. He was calling out to me and saying things in a derogatory way. He didn't run up or get too close, staying back about five feet. He had a lot of anger and was throwing rocks (not really at me, but towards me, I was not hit). I intuitively knew that he did not have good intentions and I was frightened. As I said, I was alone and didn't know anyone who I could go to. The town was so little I don't believe there was a police station and there were not a lot of tourists. Not knowing what else to do I wandered through the town and tried to lose him, eventually I went into the museum and spent some time safely in there. When I came out hours later, he was nowhere around. I was on my way back to the campsite at the end of the day, again out of nowhere he showed up. It was unnerving because it felt like he had been stationed somewhere, waiting. Still walking a few feet back behind me he again started saying some really horrible things. I don't remember exactly what he was saying but it wasn't nice and I was scared. My intuition and my body's reaction kicked in and I was looking around my environment for options and answers.

Surprisingly as I was making my way towards the riverboat dock, a huge tourist bus pulls up beside me. I was walking towards it and a woman jumps out. She had red hair, wasn't very tall and had a couple of cameras around her neck. I walked up to her and I asked if I could walk with her. I told her that the guy behind me had been following me all day and I couldn't shake him. She said yes of course I could walk with her. She was from Australia and was on tour here. We chatted and the guy took off. We boarded the ferry and crossed the river on the riverboat. She was really funny and nice and took lots of photos of the scenery. When we got to the other side I was distracted, as I wanted to hurriedly make my way to my campsite and some security. I was safe and I had been looked after. I knew then that I had angels.

The next day I asked the riverboat driver where do the big busses that cross the river go? He asked me what I was talking about. I said it again, "The big tourist bus that had the people on it from Australia. Where do they go?" He looked at me like I was nuts and said that there was no tourist bus and that the busses can't go across on his little riverboat. Hmmm, that was weird! Even though I knew she was an angel and had kept me safe, I didn't realize the extent of that encounter until much later. Eventually, I realized that the entire exchange had been not only divine but that she was truly an angel. A protector, I recognized that the Divine had sent that bus to make it look believable and that there were angels here protecting me.

One of the best ways to know if you are on the right track is to tap into your body's vibrations. When you think about the decision you need to make where do you feel it in your body? What are the sensations that you are feeling? Does it feel good and calm; do you feel inspired and thrilled? Are you energized and does your body feel strong, or are you feeling anxious with a deep knowing that this isn't for you? When we make a decision that is in alignment with our beliefs we get a calm feeling over our senses. It can show up as a relaxed stomach and central nervous system or it may show up as excitement and passion. At some point of the decision you may experience self doubt and question yourself, but if you stay connected, your senses will tell you loud and clear if the decision to go forward is correct for you.

When it is not a good decision your body will also let you know. You may get a churning or an upset feeling in your stomach, you may feel tightness in your jaw, fist, chest, or you may feel it in your throat or back, neck or across your forehead. Our posture can change and we may feel less grounded and unfocused on regular tasks. There may be an array of sensations that are familiar to you and it is through practice and connecting with these vibrations that will tell you what they mean.

Imagine a time that you were sure about the decision you were making and note the sensations that you felt in your body at that time. Did you feel more confident and have a little straighter posture? What were the feelings in your jaw, head, stomach and back? Did you feel passionate about your decision and what you were going to do? When we move ourselves into a space where we can fully trust the signs that we are getting from our gut instinct, our body and intuition, it will have a huge impact on how we live our life. We will have confidence to move directly towards what we want to create.

All of this recognition allows you to go into your internal self to make assessment. It keeps us out of external forces to help us live a full and fulfilling life. It takes us to a place where we are connecting to our inner self and our higher soul to live on our path.

When we look to outside influences to help us live, it puts us into a position where we have little or no control. We go into a cycle of giving up and blaming others for our circumstances and not creating the life that we dream of. Remember that only you can know for sure what your soul is saying and how you will be enhanced by what you do and the choices you make.

It can be daunting making some decisions as we struggle going back and forth until sometimes we no longer get to make the decision. Have you ever noticed how eventually some life changes get made for us and a choice is no longer available? You may catch your husband cheating, even though you wanted to leave the relationship for years. You may get into an accident where you have to quit your job you hate and it leads you into supporting a cause that you are passionate about. The signs to make changes begin as a nudge, then they get a little louder until finally you get hit on the head and you are forced into making the life alteration.

This doesn't need to be a huge shift where you immediately quit your job or leave your marriage, but instead take a course on the career path that you would prefer. Start a small business or engage in a seva project to support your vision. Go for marriage counseling with or without your partner and begin to create a life that is fulfilling for you.

4

UTKATASANA - Chair

Confidence, Power

*U*tkatasana is a strengthening posture. In Chair pose we sit back, feeling relaxed and confident while tapping into our power. Simple to do, yet it requires focus and control. It is within this grounded and stable state where you can spotlight how to continue generating a life full of confidence and passion. Settle into your power and keep moving further into the dream that will be fulfilling and authentic. You can see the big picture now; visualize yourself standing strong in your beautiful life full of confidence and assurance. Can you imagine how your vision is benefitting your family, community and relationships? Feel sure that what you have worked so hard at will have a positive impact on society and the entire world. You have been chosen. Keep your feet solid on the ground, your gaze onto the outcome, to allow your power and influence to radiate out from your heart.

How to do it: Standing on your mat with equal space between your feet and knees. Bend your knees sitting back as if in a chair. Arms can be on your hips, straight out in front or up to the sky. Keep your weight back towards your heels. Find a focal point and breath.

*A*lways the student, I have spent a lot of time studying and learning; yoga, meditation, the chakra system, counseling, ways to live in optimal health and how to live on purpose. All of this training and insight has given me tools to use to combat feeling overwhelmed, insecure or afraid. I love to learn and to hear what others have to say. All of these teachings help us to maintain a confidence and ability to keep moving forward within an enjoyable and sustainable workload. Connect to your own resources and power to continue confidently towards your projects and goals.

Remember the importance of getting enough rest, meditation, eating a healthy diet with drinking plenty of fresh water, exercising and deep-breathing to keep you connected to your soul and to sustain the power you need to achieve your goals. Call upon whatever supports you have available to you and enlist the help of a life-coach, counselor or spiritual director.

We all have friends and family members who want only the best for us. However, it's ideal to get an objective point of view by enlisting a professional. The benefits can be huge and direct since you get a specific amount of time intended solely towards your growth. Coaches and counselors have tools to help you break through and advance towards what you are doing without an invested interest in the outcome of your endeavor. When we are reaching for something new, the people who love us will ask themselves "how will this affect me?" They will respond in a way that will either encourage your next step or cause you to question what you are doing. To keep moving forward you will NEED to recruit people who will ask you the hard questions in a supportive way, all the while encouraging you to keep striving.

Those who achieve their dreams and continue to live on purpose do so with the help of others. When you have a support person it will help you increase your awareness, allowing you to look at the same situation with new eyes. When you are in the midst of pursuing your dream, limiting beliefs will surface, so with the help of your counselor you will be able to confidently move through them. See the benefits of reaching out for support to keep you from getting stuck by roadblocks. Be able to change directions and connect with like-minded people who are inspiring and courageous.

See all challenges as opportunities for growth containing insight. When you see a challenge, notice if you feel fearful and does that fear make you want to run away from it? Check in with your fear response, draw your energy back, tap into the courage needed to move into the new and decide clearly if this is something that your soul desires.

In 2009, I went to hear the Dali Lama speak. It was an incredible opportunity that I will cherish for the rest of my life. I went with my sister Vicky and a couple of friends. I loved the energy in the packed stadium; I loved the respect and the esteem of the experience. I felt impacted and proud by the rituals that Canada brought to him in representation of our diverse cultures as well as the ritual he brought to us.

Every person in the stadium was given a white scarf; we crossed our arms and held onto the scarves of the people beside us. The facility held 15,000 people and as we each held a connection to the persons beside us, we were able to see and feel the connection to every person in The Saddledome Stadium. The Dali Lama's speech was incredible as he spoke of his purpose and the amazing work that he is doing in the world. He spoke that each of us can take a part in helping our world; since we are all connected we can all make a difference.

One of the most profound things he said, was that we need to have confidence to have compassion. This statement really hit home for me and I continue to think about it. Notice when you are able to give someone an authentic and heartfelt compliment. This is a direct reflection of you showing confidence and feeling good enough about yourself to do so. When we can encourage and support others in their businesses, parenting, relationships and lives, when we can tell our friends and sisters that they are doing a good job, it is a mirror image of our life and accomplishments.

When we feel good about how we are showing up in the world, we have the capacity of compassion towards others. When we suffer from low self-esteem, lose our power and aren't happy about our lives, we will not have compassion for other people. We get judgmental and negative because we aren't happy within our own lives and ourselves. Create your best life ever, change any negative thoughts into a positive and enjoy all the aspects of your life. When I am in a less compassionate state I remember his words and question my confidence level.

5

BALASANA - Child

Humility, Protection

*B*alasana is a gentle pose that is pure and humble. In child's pose we surrender and protect ourselves. This is a reminder to care for you with loving thoughts and actions. Is there a person or situation in your life that is not serving your highest good? Are you allowing your thoughts and memories to debilitate you and take your energy and confidence? Guard against circumstances or people who may be sabotaging your efforts and authentic self. Trust your instincts and stay safe. Treat yourself as you would a beautiful and precious child by eating nurturing food and taking a nap. Be gentle and accepting with yourself, know your limits. Create a loving support team with positive and loving affirmations: "I am safe and supported."

How to do it: Kneeling on your yoga mat, open your knees slightly. Remaining seated on your heels, lower your forehead to the floor. Bring your hands back to your feet and breathe slowly. Modification: stack your hands and place your forehead on your hands.

*W*hen I was a single mother with two young babies I was in a place where I had to count every penny. Many days I was afraid that I didn't have enough money to buy food. It was a scary time and I felt really bad about myself. Even though I was well supported by my family and friends, I was embarrassed that I was in such a low place and I didn't want to tell anyone that I wasn't sure how I was going to feed the kids. I was ashamed that I had allowed my life to get so messed up. I was a single mother working 2 jobs raising my three-year-old son Forrester and three-month-old daughter Chloe.

I worked running a licensed day home in my house. After all the children were picked up, I would get my own children fed, bathed and in bed before heading out to clean offices until after midnight. It was a struggle, but I was very grateful to have the support of my mom and sister who came and babysat my kids while I went out to clean at night.

Magic showed up at a time when I was most desperate and I will never forget it. On my way to my second job I stopped to pick up a few groceries for the next day. I was happy that my Mom was staying with my children and I relished getting out of the house for a few hours alone.

At the grocery store I was armed with a calculator to get as much food as possible without exceeding the twenty dollars in my purse. I needed to feed the day home children the next few days, as well as my own. As I pushed my cart into a new aisle I noticed that there was no one else in the aisle, this was pretty unusual for this very busy grocery store. While pushing my cart up the aisle I saw something on the ground, walking closer I saw that it was a bundle of money. I couldn't believe it! I bent down, picked it up and literally raised it towards the sky and said "thank-you". Overwhelmed and close to tears with gratitude and the knowing that the divine was looking out for me. Gingerly walking around the store looking to see if anyone had lost any money, there was no one that I could find. I asked at the front counter if anyone had asked about losing anything and again nothing. I knew deep, deep in my soul that, that money had been a direct gift from Spirit. I was not proud of my poverty and I felt shame being in such desperate need. This is a place I do not ever want to re-visit, it did however, reaffirm a faith to me which I cherish and forced me to walk fully into humility and simplicity.

Since I now live in a place of abundance I enjoy paying it forward. I have always had a soft spot for young mothers all around the world who work hard to feed their families. There was one occasion, not too long ago where I was standing in the grocery store line up behind a young mom. She had two children in the grocery cart and a book full of coupons. I was hugely impressed when she was able to get her entire cartload of groceries down to twenty-seven dollars. Between handing over the coupons, dealing with her toddlers and packing her own groceries, she could not find her wallet. I said, "don't worry, just add it onto my bill." She of course was reluctant at first and continued to look for her wallet and debit card. I said, "Really, I am so impressed that you got it down so low, plus I remember being a young mom myself. Please let me get this for you." The cashier stared at me and I nodded to start to ring my order in. The young mom thanked me and carried on. I will never know her story and I don't know how that experience affected her, but I do know that I will do it again and again.

Support happened for me a second time, coming directly from my parents, Joyce and Garth. I have always been extremely close to my parents and knew that they were there for me. I wanted to raise my children as I had been raised because they were such a fantastic example of love, caring and partnership, with an ability to honor and respect each other's individuality.

I went to visit them one evening and when I was leaving their home my mom had compiled a very large sack of groceries. They had added not only food but luxury items such as Kleenex and paper towels. Facial tissue was an item I considered unnecessary and didn't purchase since I had toilet paper that would work just as well. I was so moved and thankful for the items and as I was getting ready to leave, my dad came out and added a bottle of his homemade wine to my bag.

The generosity, gratitude and humility I felt were huge. I recognized that they knew I was doing my best in a very unfortunate situation plus they understood and accepted me. I walked out to my car, put the kids into their car seats, stored the groceries in the trunk and I cried. I cried with relief that they saw what I was going through without judging me, I cried because I had their support and I felt extremely comforted in their holding me up.

Getting divorced felt like such a failure, I felt disgrace that I wasn't able to make my marriage work. I felt like my life was a mess and it was difficult to bear the humiliation. I was embarrassed and I was dealing with a lot. Some people were supportive and understanding, and then there were others who were not. I allowed the negative judgment to push me even further down because I was already feeling so crappy about myself all on my own.

How often do you find yourself around people or in a situation that you know is not serving your highest good? You leave a meeting or a visit and you feel low, tired and drained. Though it is not always possible, easy or even probable, consider ridding yourself of the people that you believe are holding you down. Limit time that you spend with people who are sabotaging your efforts and who are not able to support you. I believe that if we can reduce the amount of time that we spend with them and shrink the effect they a have on us, we will be better able to stay with our intentions.

Keep coming back to your intention, create a purpose statement and affirm it each and every day. When you recognize negative comments or limitations, go back to your affirmations. "I am a strong and capable person." "I easily and effortlessly move forward into my purpose." Tell your angels that it is safe for you to move into your intention and ask your angels to gently guide or even push you towards your goals. Do NOT believe the limiting programming that you got as a child, the sabotage from others or the nay sayers. Surround yourself with encouraging, compassionate, like-minded and reputable people who support you to stay true to you and your intentions.

6
BADDHA KONASANA – Cobbler/Butterfly

Opening, Transformation

*B*addha **Kanasana** is an opening yoga posture. Cobbler or Butterfly pose allows you to relax and release as you expand. Open yourself now to new relationships, situations, and opportunities for change. We are always in a state of flux; we are constantly aging, growing, and transforming. This posture signifies that there is transformation taking place in your mind, body, or spirit that will impact your life. When we hang on to jobs, relationships, or situations that are no longer serving our highest good, then drama arises. If we simply allow the order of change to take place it can be smooth, exciting and pleasant. Nature is an excellent example of the ease of change. The cycle and seasons continuously bring rebirth and death. Embrace growth and expansion fearlessly. Open yourself up to transformation.

How to do it: Sitting on your mat, bring the soles of your feet together and gently pull your heels in towards you. Place your hands behind your back onto the floor and lift yourself up slightly so that you are sitting tall. Next, bring your hands forward to hold your toes with your fingers, press your thumb into the pad below your big toe. Take slow steady breaths.

We never really know where we are going and what the universe has in store for us. As much as we visualize and set intentions, the truth is that we will be guided on our path. We believe we know what we want and how to get it, yet intentions can limit our visions. Sometimes we can't dream big enough for ourselves and want to squeeze our dream into our present reality. When we keep moving towards being of service, having connection and a life that is purposeful, opportunities will unfold that will be even more amazing than we ever could have believed.

I was taking Advanced Leadership Training at the Omega Institute in Rhinebeck, New York, USA so I could hold Yoga in Action Workshops in my community. Workshops in my community. I wanted very much to teach their curriculum, and was working diligently towards that. In their training they emphasize the importance of having a partner when running these workshops. While I was at the training I kept rolling this around in my mind, wondering whom I could ask to be my partner. When I was in Savasana I kept asking Spirit, who should be my partner, who would make a good partner? A name kept popping into my mind, yet I dismissed it just as quickly. I thought no, I didn't think this would be something that would interest the person who kept coming to me.

Fifteen minutes later I was standing in the line for the washroom and a woman (another Canadian) said to me, "I think I did the Yoga for Cancer Survivors training with you a few years ago." I replied, "Yes, I did that training." We chatted about the course and what we were doing for cancer survivors. Then she asked, "Where in Canada do you live?" I told her and her next sentence was "I know a yoga instructor there." I replied "Oh really, who?" When she told me, she said the same name that had come to me in Savasana. I did not get an opportunity to talk to her again that weekend, but I knew without a shadow of a doubt who my new partner was going to be to teach Yoga in Action.

I trusted that the universe knew what it was doing; I was remaining open, even though I was completely apprehensive as to how well we would work together. With all the doubt I continued to trust the guidance and reached out to her as soon as I got home. I wanted desperately to evolve the yoga I was teaching and I was ready for a transformation of my offerings and myself. I knew that I couldn't do it on my own, that co-creation was what was needed and I trusted in the divine guidance. When I came home and I approached her, with her own apprehensions to working with me, she decided it was exactly what she was looking for.

Within three months she went and did her training and we started facilitating the workshops. We spent the next several years teaching a curriculum that not only had a huge impact and benefit to our participants but we both continued to transform and grow. Each session we were exposed to new ways of seeing ourselves, dug deep into the inner work and grew through collaboration. As much as I wanted to extend myself initially on my own, I stayed open to co-create my dreams with the explicit help from the Divine. These experiences are something you have to go through to move you to a different energetic and vibration field, to transform. It was perfect. Thank-you Spirit, I am so glad I listened.

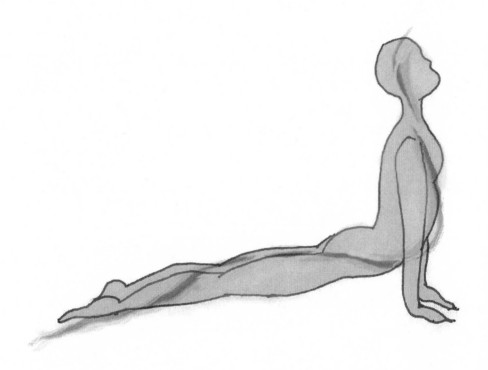

7

BHUJANGASANA - Cobra

Unity, Shadow

*B*hujangasana posture implies that there is a continuous flow of energy from feminine to masculine to feminine... This gives us an opportunity to see ourselves in others. Typically we see masculine energy as task and goal oriented, assertive, competitive and analytical. While feminine energy is viewed as emotional, creative, passionate and intuitive. Where are you at right now? Do you find a need to get more in touch with your creativity and feelings or are you at a place where you need to strategize and assert yourself in a situation? We all possess qualities of both the masculine and feminine energies, determine how balanced yours are right now. Though we want to be productive and achieve, remember to also allow time to go with the flow, noticing if you judge some of these aspects as your shadow. Acknowledging our shadow (unwelcome) emotions allows us to shine a light on them. When we shine a light on a shadow it disappears.

How to do it: Lie on your stomach, with your hands on the floor beside your chest, press palms and the tops of your feet firmly into the floor. Slide gently forward and lift your chest off the floor. Keep your gaze forward and breathe deeply.

*I*n our world there are all types of duality that exist within each of us and all aspects of the universe. We believe in good and bad, we cannot experience happiness with never having felt sadness. There is Yin and Yang, strength and weakness, up and down, open and closed, positive and negative.

Shakti is the smooth, creative feminine energy that activates the emotional power, our passion, as well as empathy and nurturing selves. Shiva symbolizes the conscious energy of completing tasks and goals with determination and competition. Since we all possess both masculine and feminine qualities, let's not misinterpret them as positive or negative. What we need to look at is if we are living with these energies balanced or are we pushing against our true nature. I know when I move into dealing with tasks with a more masculine energy I feel like I am pushing against the flow. It literally feels like I have to shoulder myself against a locked door. I will keep setting goals, and assert myself in ways to get things accomplished. When I finally say enough allow myself off the hook and leave to go meditate, I can bring myself back into balance. Then I come at the chore with a fresh, emotional and feminine perspective that works much better for me.

Carl Jung taught us that the shadow aspect of our personality is the part of us that is in conflict to our idealized self. We can determine if a quality is a shadow when we find ourselves wanting to hide it from others, we feel judged for it or it threatens our survival. Sometimes we don't want others to see us cry, and we believe it is a sign of weakness. Perhaps we believe we need to be quiet because our shadow is that we want to be loud and the center of attention. Maybe our shadow shows up as jealousy, anger, neediness, panic, depression or despair. Our shadow is not in alignment with the image we want to portray to the world.

The beautiful thing about the shadow is that every one of us has them. We all have aspects of ourselves that we don't want others to see. Our shadow can prevent us from taking risks and from thinking of ourselves as worthy. It is beneficial to keep coming back to the knowledge that we ALL have a shadow, yet we have people in our lives who we accept and cherish, shadows and all. If we all have a shadow and we don't judge others because of their shadow, then it gives us hope to stop judging ourselves for our own shadow. Yes, sometimes we get angry, jealous, needy and emotional. Sometimes we have outbursts and don't like our behavior, but let's all cut our self some slack, embrace our imperfections, and accept others for theirs.

As we continue to accept both our masculine and feminine energies, our Shiva and our Shakti, how do we remain empowered to live our life fully with balanced masculine and feminine? Determine when you are coming at your life more from a masculine perspective. You are making lists; using your "power move" to get things accomplished, setting time lines, feeling competitive and driven. How is it working for you? Are you getting a lot accomplished? Does it feel like you are moving with the flow or like you are swimming upstream? What are the sensations in your body; do you notice any discomfort or tightness in your muscles? Meditate on what you want to accomplish and how you are going to do it. If this doesn't feel like a place that is comfortable and with ease, notice if you might not be in balance and are instead coming at tasks, decisions and goals from a more masculine perspective. Come at your life with creativity, feminine energy, stop making lists, remove the competitive motivation and move into a more relaxed state connecting to your emotions and feelings. Meditate to hear the voice of your intuition and establish how you want life to feel.

Perhaps you are coming at your life with more feminine energy where you are creative, emotional and nurturing. However, you don't feel like you are able to get tasks done, you get taken advantage of and unsuccessfully trying to please everyone. Now you recognize a need to increase your masculine energy into your projects, decisions and tasks by creating boundaries and finding an ability to say "NO". Now would be a good time to establish lists, set time based goals and find your competitive edge. Practice saying "no" and take time before you answer someone's requests. Again, check in with your body and decide for yourself if you want to do it or not. Meditate to increase your masculine power, visualize your strength and command, tap into your fire and stand up for yourself.

Keep these energies balanced so as to go with the flow confidently. Move through your life with ease and strength to accomplish what you want to do. Use your creativity, your analytical mind and your emotions to make choices that serve you, your family and your higher self. Use your beautiful nurturing skills to nurture those who you love most and add yourself to the top of the list.

8

SAVASANA - Corpse

Rest, Recovery

S avasana is the most important of all the yoga postures. The purpose of Corpse pose is to heal muscles that have been worked with asana, and prepare for meditation. Connecting with earth's energy through rest is important in maintaining sustainability and our complete wellbeing. Relaxation helps us to maintain weight, cope and heal by decreasing our stress. In North America a large percentage of our population is sleep deprived. Are you getting enough sleep? You have the ability to have the life that you desire, it is coming to you at this moment, just remember to stay effective by getting proper rest to recover from stress. Get thirty more minutes of sleep each night and notice an overall change in your life.

How to do it: Lie down on your back. Make sure you are warm and comfortable. Remove your glasses and start by taking three long, slow, smooth breaths. Move your head from side to side so it is comfortable. Your arms are at your sides without touching your body with your palms facing up. Allow your feet to gently flop open to the sides.

I was once asked, "Candace I have known you for a long time. I have been taking your yoga classes for many years and you never miss a class, you never come in upset or frustrated. I keep waiting for something in your life to shake you, to break you down and I've never seen it happen. How come that is? How do you stay healthy, positive and happy?" This question really stuck with me. Of course there have been many, many times when I have been shaken; I definitely get unhappy, negative and not feeling well. I absolutely get scared, absorbed in self-doubt and questioning "what's the point?" and I most certainly have cried about my relationships. So, what's different? How can I keep coming into class every day feeling happy and calm? I rest and give myself a chance to recover.

I know what to do to maintain optimal health, and although I don't always do it, I identify when to come back to my regime. Sleep is one of the first things to do for health. When you feel even the beginning of a cold or flu head for bed. Add an extra half hour meditation if you need it. Take a hard look at your schedule and add more rest. The benefits will be huge.

While working in various jobs or when in school and I got sick, I would think; Yay, I'm sick, I get to have a few days of lying around, watching T.V. and having someone bring me soup. With no expectations put on me, I enjoyed a week of pajama days. Perhaps you already find you are taking a day off every other month around your period. Possibly it's normal for you to take a week off each winter for a cold and another several days for the flu. There may even be a part of you that enjoys having a week of illness to give you a break. If this is what comes up for you, then I truly believe it is time to change jobs.

Make changes so that you don't feel a need to create an illness to nurture yourself. Create a plan to take care of yourself on a regular basis. On the first day of every moon cycle don't make dinner, leave work early and go to your bed with chocolate, soup, a good book or movie. If you are no longer getting your moon cycle do this on the day of the full moon. Remember, if you don't look after yourself no one else will!

Clear examples of mind/body connection showed up after my separation. I was running two businesses, paying a mortgage, and looking after my young children. Of course, I was under tremendous stress. The stress showed up in my body through illness and disease. I went through a year of monthly bouts of strep throat (holding in angry words), I developed gallstones (resentment, bitterness) and then I got shingles waiting for the other shoe to drop (fear, tension). Every month around the time of my moon cycle I got sick and ended up at the Doctor's with strep throat. Just before my ex-husband moved out, I developed gallstones and had my gallbladder removed. It was a debilitating and almost unbearable year.

Take a hard look at what is going on in your life when you get ill. It is imperative to look at how we deal with stress and how we maintain our immune system. Whenever I get an illness, aches or pains I check in with what is going on all around me. Illness is not caused by one specific belief, trauma or situation, but we can look at the whole picture of what is going on in our life. Connecting to your intuition ask the difficult question, "What do I need to change in my lifestyle?" "What do I need to add or remove from my daily routine?" "How are my reactions to situations compounding this illness?" With rest and recovery we can build ourselves back up to optimal health.

9

NATARAJASANA - Dancer

Grace, Aura

*N*atarajasana posture is a beautiful pose, which embodies grace, poise and charm. The Dance in you radiates an etheric light of a luminescent colorful glow. Dance through your life and love all the radiance that you emanate. Embrace your environment, colors, beauty and find pleasure in all of your activities. Do, buy and encase yourself with only what you truly adore. When you surround yourself with grace it absorbs into every cell of your being with your connection to the Divine. Love and compassion pours out from your every fiber and people around you will respond to your aura. Are you able to see auras? Can you close your eyes and see colors? Many will not be able to articulate what they are feeling and seeing but will perceive your magnetism just as you will perceive others. Remain free and giving with your love while projecting your glorious light.

How to do it: Stand on your mat. Bend your right knee. Reach your right hand back and clasp the inside of your right ankle. Inhale; reach your left hand up to the sky. Exhale as you gently draw your right foot away from your body. Breathe smoothly. Repeat on the other side.

A few years ago I went to India on a spiritual pilgrimage. We were a small group of seven women entering a life altering experience. Given the opportunity to explore the powerful feminine energies of Yogini's from the Hindu religion. It was magnificent and emotional as we connected to the divine on various levels. In some circumstances the energy was chaotic and turbulent filled with angst. The feminine showed up as connection, faithful to sisterhood, at other times we walked into auras and energies of hesitation, uncertainty and vulnerability.

One evening after a day of connection and mystery our group gathered under the rooftop dome of the Sri Vidya Shrine at the Himalayan Institute, Khajuraho, India. We were in a healing circle and we were asked to share our impression of each other, what we were projecting to the world. I immediately shared how one of my travelling companions embodies grace, elaborating to say how she holds herself and presents herself with confidence and poise. The rest of the group agreed and she accepted this understanding with elegance. Minutes later, I learned that she has a daughter and her name is Grace – how lovely! I love dancer pose and when I think of the word grace I think of this beautiful, refined and stylish friend of mine. She is poised in her speech and every movement she makes, her aura exudes charm.

Is there someone in your life who embodies grace and an ethereal or angelic presence? Perhaps it is you who floats through life like an angel or spirit. I see dancers who have these beautiful qualities where they make their movements so incredibly striking doing it seemingly effortlessly. They bring an ease and quality that makes you think that you could do it too. And you can.

Grace is a beautiful thing and often the people who I see who are full of grace aren't even aware of it. Acknowledge the graceful qualities in you! Where and when do they show up? Are you graceful when you are looking after your children? Are you full of grace when you are in a conversation with a close and dear friend? Cooking a beautiful meal? Doing the books or the banking? Or when you are making love? I know that I am full of grace when I teach Yoga. It is when I make it look easy, when I am authentic and full of love and joy. I bring grace through with the words I use and the experience that I create for participants; it is when students can most clearly see my aura. So again, think about when you are full of charm and kindness, recognize when you are authentic and simplistic. It is when you are composed and fluid as you flow through life making your labors look easy and effortless.

10

ADHO MUKHA SVANASANA - Downward Facing Dog

Routine, Efficiency

*A*dho Mukha Svanasana is about taking stock of your daily routine. Downward Facing Dog posture is a reminder to think about what needs to be faced and dealt with. Is there a task you have been putting off? What gets done each and every day? Do you find yourself chasing your tail? Take a deep breath to find ease and joy with the mundane everyday tasks of life. Live in the present moment full of pride and satisfaction. Set an intention, make a list, create a plan, and maintain a routine. Many of us would prefer to be on vacation and living adventures, but the reality is that most of our life is spent doing the same thing each day. Embrace everyday activities full of gratitude and satisfaction. Efficiently accomplish all that needs to get done as an effective use of energy, and then rush to the parts of your life that you're passionate about. Rest your body and your mind in the ease of the familiar.

How to do it: Come onto your hands and knees then curl your toes under. Take your knees off of the mat as you lift your sitting bones up towards the sky. Make sure your hands are shoulder width apart with your fingers spread to take your weight off of your wrists, now breathe smoothly.

*W*hat do you do every day that you enjoy and what do you dread? Is there something in your life that you would like to add to your daily routine that you believe would help you to maintain balance and pleasure with everyday tasks? Would you like to increase your connection to spirit? Would you feel healthier if you added more vegetables and fruits into your diet? Would you like to see yourself drinking more water and consuming less caffeine? How about boosting your exercise program or yoga practice? Now is the time to take a look at what you are doing and why you aren't adding in the things that bring you joy and satisfaction. Remind yourself of what makes life a little easier and more fulfilling.

Tricks to get started:

1. Set a timer and stick to it. When the timer goes off, finish up thinking "Huh that was easy!"
2. Set the stage for a pleasant and comfortable environment. Light a candle or bring in flowers.
3. Reward yourself with what brings you joy and nourishes your soul. "Yay, I did it!"

Some people naturally want to get the boring things in life done quickly so that they can go out and play. Others are procrastinators and drag tasks out making them even more dreadful. Whatever your personality type, when we have a time crunch we all usually rise to the occasion and get it done.

As human's we often don't do what we really want to be doing. Why? We offer valid reasons, yet we know a lot are excuses. My suggestion is to not look at the entire list. I propose deciding which one of those changes you want to add in the most and then go for it. If you want to add twenty minutes of daily yoga practice start with five minutes, the next day do ten, slowly working your way up to twenty minutes. Continue to add it in each day for three weeks. If some days you only stretch your arms to the sky, connect to your breath and do a forward bend that is perfectly okay.

Make a commitment to yourself and don't let yourself down. Every time we break a promise it hurts the relationship a little bit more. Enlist others to do it with you such as friends, family members or reach out on social media. Commit to your soul and remind yourself how worth it you are.

I love and respect Caroline Myss, who says she meets with her own spiritual director every week for two hours. Successful people of this world are the ones who are willing to continue to learn, fail, grow and heal themselves. It is important for us to not only talk the talk but to truly walk the walk.

How can we add more joy into our life and still get everything done that we need to do each day? I like to prioritize:

1. Should Do's

The Should Do's, are those things that we guilt ourselves into doing. Take a look at your "should's". Do you really need to do them? Does it matter if you don't do them? Can you change a "should" into "I get to"? When we are doing things because we think we should, but don't want to, it creates resentment. By re-categorizing them into a "get to", we are tapping into our gratitude and abundant way of thinking. So, let's plan on bypassing the "should" do list.

Running or exercising can sometimes be a place where people think it is something that they should do. Again find some pleasure in it. I look forward to listening to certain songs, getting outside, challenging myself and being with Coal, my dog. Doing the dishes, my husband is great at making dishwashing time fun for the whole family. He tells jokes or gets everyone singing songs and we hear about their day. In fact, nobody really truly wants to miss out on dishes at our house.

2. Need to Do's

Now focus on getting the Need to Do's done as fast as possible. What in your life do you "need to do", that you don't love doing? Sometimes my inner five-year-old comes out. I want to stamp my feet and yell, "I don't want to do this!" How can you make the experience more fun and extra pleasant so that you will want to get at it? I play games with myself to make these tasks more enjoyable so they don't become drudgery, plus it keeps me from procrastinating too long. I create a plan to make the situation as pleasant as I can so that I will enjoy the experience.

Bookwork is still when I procrastinate the most. I have done all of our businesses books for years and I get a lot of mileage out of complaining that I have to do them. Most of my friends, as well as my mentor told me that I should hire a bookkeeper. I finally got to the point where I spoke to our accountant to tell him that we needed to get a bookkeeper. He told me "but you're so good at it!" Well that was all I needed. I have embraced the part of my personality that is good at doing books; I enjoy reevaluating where our money is going and take a look at our investments. I make the experience as pleasurable as possible with yummy coffees, chocolate, music and candles. I procrastinate less and feel proud of what I do year after year for our family.

3. Want to Do's

Then we can get to the Want to Do's. Mostly I live by the phrase "if it isn't fun, don't do it". There was a time when I didn't love driving my children around to all of their activities. I would be in the middle of something, or would have to rush from place to place and things would be forgotten. Not long into these activities I changed my perspective and instead saw the fun in it. Let's face it, it's not like I had to do the activity, many times it was a drop, "Bye sweetie, have fun, see you at seven o'clock" and off I would zoom. These were times that we got to chat, catch up and listen to a special song. I got to hear about their day at school, what was going on with their friends and what their challenges were with the activity I was taking them to.

When this change of perspective started I also changed my language at the same time. I began saying, "get to" instead of "have to". "I look forward to taking my daughter to gymnastics, I'm inspired when I do our books and I feel great after going for a run." Give it a try, say it out loud to the people around you and see if you notice a difference.

11

GARUDASANA – Eagle

G **arudasana** is a yoga posture that requires you to pay attention. While doing this posture notice any messages coming to you from your body or through your third eye. We receive messages from Spirit all the time and in many ways. Have there been any signs or symbols showing themselves to you lately? Notice which animals keep showing up, random dimes you find, rainbows, flowers, birds, butterflies, lights flickering, repetitive numbers or certain smells. Have you been having a recurring dream? Spirit answers us in many ways, we just need to acknowledge and accept the messages. Allow your body to be a conduit for signals coming to you. Now is the time to ask your question, watch for a sign, and be aware of a message from the Divine.

How to do it: Stand on your mat with your knees slightly bent. Wrap your right leg around your left leg. Now place your left elbow inside your right elbow and wrap your arms around. Extend your thumbs to your third eye and look up.

y ou are walking along the parking lot, heading into the bank and you look down and you see a crow's feather. You pause and bend down to pick it up. That is a sign. You don't know how you noticed it and you don't know why you were drawn to pick it up, yet you did.

You are sitting and talking with a friend and a butterfly lands on your arm, you continue chatting. The butterfly flies around and lands again and by the third landing you find yourself telling your friend a story about your grandmother. That is a sign, and specifically a sign from your grandmother.

I smell cigarette smoke when my paternal grandmother comes to me. She used to smoke in a way that I found fascinating. She would half exhale it out and then inhale it again and the smoke would float around between her mouth and nose. Whenever I do any energy work I will often smell cigarette smoke later that day and usually for a few days more. One weekend my sister came to stay at my house to attend a workshop I was teaching. Later that evening we were sitting and chatting and I said to her "Grandma's here, I can smell cigarette smoke." She said, "oh, I was wondering about that, I can smell it too."

My sister Vicky and I were making a twelve-hour journey driving to our aunt's home across the prairies. All of a sudden we looked at each and both said, "Oh, do you feel that? It's cold like we just drove through a spirit." Vicky added "Cold and it smells like dirt." Before we could finish our sentences, my sister pointed to the side of the road, there along the highway were three white crosses with flowers in reverence.

A few summers ago I started to find dimes everywhere. I would walk along and pick up a dime. This happened so often that my daughter Chloe even commented on it. Click. That was the clue that I needed to hear. Hmmm, why do I keep finding dimes?

It took me a few more months until I got clarity why I was seeing all the dimes. I was doing an on-line course and during a session we were asked to write about our spiritual development and the women in our lives who have been pivotal and influential in our spiritual growth. I recalled a story not of my grandmother, but of my grandfather. When I was a little girl my grandfather would buy warts, yes warts, from my cousins and neighborhood kids. He would pay them a dime for each of their warts. They would count up the number of warts they had, he would negotiate with them and eventually he would hand over the coins in exchange for the warts. I was fascinated that within a few weeks their warts would be gone; completely gone, without a mark left on them. Finally I got a wart, and I was excited for Grandpa to buy it from me. He looked at me and said. "You know how to can get rid of it yourself, though I'll still give you a dime." What? He didn't want my wart? It took me a while to get the message. I KNEW how to heal them myself. I knew that I just needed to believe that they were going and they would be gone.

So now I know whenever I find a dime, my grandpa is with me reminding me that I know what I am suppose to do and to keep moving forward. Since sharing this story with others, I have heard of many people finding dimes. If you keep finding dimes, recognize the chance to shift limiting and outdated beliefs. Please watch for signs, the divine is giving us messages all the time. If you are unsure, please ask for signs then pay attention for them to show up, and have fun with it.

Several years ago I started seeing hawks everywhere I went. Each time I drove any distance I would see 3 hawks along the way. One day my daughter Chloe was driving behind me and saw one of the hawks. When we stopped she said, "That was so cool, I don't think I've ever seen a hawk and he was flying right above your car!" This went on all summer long.

On Labor Day weekend in September we went camping with several other families. The weather was wet and rainy so we hung a large blue tarp across the campsite above the fire pit. One afternoon there were about twenty of us sitting around the fire. Out of nowhere a hawk flew down under the tarp, over the fire pit and hit me on the head. One of my friends shouted, "Holy shit, did you all see that? That was a hawk!" What was happening?

Though I was shocked to get hit on the head by a hawk, I knew it was a sign. Frustratingly though, I felt like I wasn't getting it, I wasn't getting the message that hawk was trying to tell me. I reached out to other healers and spiritual counselors but I was not getting any insight that resonated with me. Then I was speaking with a student/friend after yoga class and she said, "YOU are the messenger. You are the one that's teaching and counseling, bringing messages to people all the time."

I realized that I was often editing messages, that for several months now I had been going through my own transformation yet I was not sharing my insight with others. Seeing hawks reminds me to give messages as I hear them, not sensor them or decide not to say them. I was the messenger. This was the validation that I needed to allow myself to share and channel.

It was a couple of years later that I decided to participate in the Global Seva Challenge India and the hawks began to appear again. I would see them often but especially when I was making decisions about what to do. It felt comforting and it felt like I was on the right track when I would see a hawk. That is until the full moon the night before the winter solstice 2013.

I was awake during the night, which is common for me on the night of the full moon. I was upstairs in my office/loft when I heard something that was an unusual sound. I wasn't sure what the noise was but it made me get up and investigate as a shiver ran through my body. The next morning my son Forrester looked out the dining room door and said "What on earth?" I ran to look and a hawk had flown into our house and had fallen dead on our upper deck. There was a light layer of snow on the deck with no other markings or footprints in the snow. The bird lay on his back with wings drawn in, but surrounding the hawk was a snow angel that he had made in the snow before he transitioned. I am heartsick as I write this; it feels very emotional to me. I know that I now fully embody hawk spirit and am honored and blessed to have Hawk as my totem.

Remain open and willing for transformation to happen and be receptive to opportunities and guidance. Every New Years instead of making a resolution, I like to create an intention for myself. This intention needs to be easy to remember, one or two words, so that I can keep bringing it back to myself throughout the year.

One year my intention was to increase my intuition, so for that entire year I taught all of my yoga classes intuitively. It was quite an experience. I was used to planning out my classes, creating a flow. I would write out the intention of the class, the teachings, the postures and a meditation or a reading for Savasana. I love to study yoga each day and I found it fulfilling to plan my classes.

It was uncomfortable at first to go into a class unprepared and to just follow what came to me. However, as a result I received a lot of positive feedback. It was during that year that I encountered validation that my intuition was accurate. Almost every day after class, students would come up and tell me they thought I was talking directly to them. One student said that when she felt I was speaking right into her ear she knew the message was for her; when I sounded further away she knew the message was for someone else. That was the validation that I needed and it moved me to continue to listen and believe more strongly in my intuition.

After the year was up I went back to planning my yoga classes, however I continued to say things during the class that pop into my head. I went back to planning my yoga sequences and designing a theme to my week of classes. I find my classes are more interesting for me when I do it that way. The beauty though is that I continue to add messages for my students.

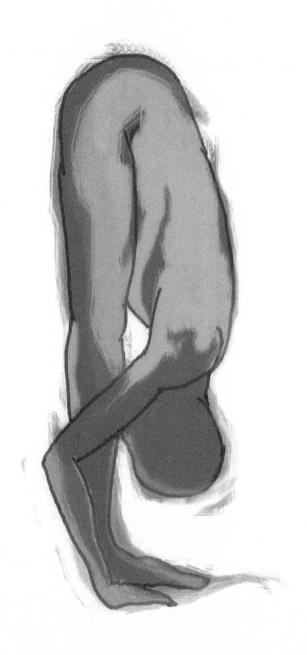

12

UTTANASANA - Forward Bend

Reflective, Spiritual Shift

*U*ttanasana is a yoga posture that encourages reflection as you move into a spiritual shift. Forward Bend is not as physical as other postures, but in the gentlest of movement we find strength and insight. This is a time in your life where you are undergoing or anticipating a spiritual change, where you may be feeling apprehensive and unsure. Often when we go through something like this we experience feelings of reflection, sadness and loss. Treat yourself reverently and uphold introspection. Take time to walk in nature, sit in the sun, turn off the news and follow your thoughts and emotions without judgment. Meditate twice each day. When you are shifting spiritual change and growth, your body requires kindness and compassion.

How to do it: Stand on your mat, inhale and lift your arms to the sky. Exhale extending your arms out to the side as you bend forward. Keep your back as flat as possible for as far as you can, rounding when you bring your fingers toward your toes, add a bend in your knees if needed. Relax in this posture by bringing your thumbs to the inside of your elbows and let your head hang inside the square or place your hands on the floor.

We live in worlds that are filled with so much doing that we can't hear what our soul is asking of us. We feel disconnected and unhappy so we add in more doing to fill the space and try to fill a need. We stay in horrible jobs that we work at all day long, then we rush to yoga or fitness classes, eat poorly, veg out in front of the T.V. or computer screen and then do it all over again the next day. Then one day we get hit with a thought or are guided by an event that makes us sit up and take note.

What is a spiritual shift? This comes to us as knowingness; a spiritual growth. These shifts can be large or small. They can be life altering and in some cases life shattering or they can be quick, little changes in our energy. We know something to be truth yet we don't know how we know it. Maybe they are childhood lessons, past life intuitions or maybe not, but when we go through a shift the lessons will come rapidly. We get the message several times within a few days or weeks. Messages may come as people in your life, people past, or new people come in with a message. It might be in the form of an email, a message on social media or someone you bump into. You come across challenges or experiences that seem to have the same theme. You get obvious signs or dreams and memories that bombard you.

Spiritual shifts want you to make changes in your life so that you will be happy and joyful. However, we can ONLY hear spiritual guidance when we get quiet. When we stop filling our days with busyness and be silent, meditate and reflect then we will shift.

I can see spiritual shifts when I look back, so clearly. Can you see how each event has guided you on your course? One event at a time like when we were in pre-school holding onto a string, but this thread leads us from birth to death through all our connections. This web connects us to all the other people and experiences in our lives, some of which can be quick little encounters that make a large impact on us. One person may make a flippant comment, you take it to heart and it creates reflection and spiritual growth. It is those comments that come from an earth angel that spark you to another level in your life, towards another challenge and into a new thought process. This person might be a spiritual counselor, a mentor or beloved teacher, yet it also might be someone you chat with in a coffee shop that you don't know and never see again. You might have an encounter with someone while standing in a line-up or a cashier in the drive through. You never know when it will hit or how it will change you. Spiritual shifts also come from experiences that you undergo. As you know, experiences can seem relatively simple yet you feel a massive energetic shift. You may be in a place where the energy is vibrating very high or alternately very low and this has a profound effect on your body and mind.

How can we live in this world, in our body, with our family, our belief system and social pressures fully happy, content and joyful? The question I am asked is how can we be alive in this energetic world with all of the controversial people, places and energies and how do we do it and stay centered and grounded keeping our bodies well?

In truth, we won't always feel happy and at peace with what is going on in our homes, our surroundings, and especially with what we hear on the news, so how can we achieve a state of mental gratification and connection? Happiness is not a destination but is instead a way of life once you connect to spirit, when you get yourselves naked and strip off all of the labels and limiting beliefs that inhibit us. Sit peacefully and trustfully surrounded by dangers and feel the bond of being safe and protected, notice the energy of your own higher power that keeps you sheltered. Acknowledge the Divine as beautiful, strong, sexy, gorgeous entities protecting and guiding over you. Imagine being loved so completely and unconditionally by your Guardian Angel.

When we go through a spiritual growth, change and expansion it can be a remarkable and exciting period of our time. We want to tell our story and share it with others who we hope will understand. We have gained a knowing about ourselves and we have new insight into how we want to live in this world. We are refreshed and energized and we want to put it into practice right away. We know we are changed and will never go back to how we were before. People we see remind us of how we look different and we know that they can see our light. We can feel that our light is shining brighter and clearer.

Then we start to feel a little sad, maybe a little annoyed or unsure. We may have bouts of anger and outbursts or we may find ourselves crying and wondering what is going on. This is all a normal part of any spiritual expansion. We go through a period of mourning. We have the knowing, yet we are stepping into new territory. We may be struggling with articulating what has happened within us and we may be still living in a similar routine, surrounded with sameness. Please know that this period of anger, frustration or sadness and depression are a normal part of the growth!

We are saying goodbye to the way we were. We are letting go of very comfortable ways of living and being. We are experimenting with our new selves and we are walking into unknown territory. With each day we fear that we are getting farther away from our life changing experience. We are scared that we will just fall back into old patterns and it will have been all for naught.

I must to tell you that you can never go back to that person who you were. You have seen, felt and experienced a new way of being. You have the knowing now for what is on the horizon and for all of the potential. You are expanded and you are beautiful.

Remember that this mourning is an important part of the expansion. We need to remember who we were and we need to honor that soul. All that you are changing has worked perfectly for you for many years; it has been a blessing and an attribute of your perfectness. Though you are ready for change and it is here, we also know that the universe has a divine plan.

My advice is to remember that you are not alone. You do not have to do this alone and you are not the only person who has gone through life altering expansion. Call upon your guides both in the physical and spiritual world. Keep your knowing deep into your heart and in your soul.

Ask God and Goddess to help you and support you through this process. Call on all of your angels to support you now. Ask your runner angel to help you get the mundane done easily and effortlessly. Ask your guardian angel to support you and to help ease the pain and suffering. Ask your guardian at the gate to gently push you forward on this path. Lastly ask all your other entities to offer guidance, knowing and support so that this transition will be smooth and gentle. Remember always to hug those people closest to you and draw them into your new energy field. Share this with your lovers and friends, and remain strong in the change.

13

DEVIASANA – Goddess

Divine Feminine, Yogini

*D*eviasana pose reminds you to stand in your own personal, feminine, Goddess strength. In Goddess posture we are on strong legs with our entire body open and fierce. Are you giving your energy away? Who or what are you giving it to? How do you stay empowered in your capabilities? Surround yourself and connect with other woman who you admire and cherish. Join a class or attend a workshop where you are saturated in new beliefs and the power of the Divine Feminine. When we live in fear, we limit our experiences and our opportunities. Allow yourself to be seen as you are right now, draw your energy back into your solar plexus and take a risk. It is time to step out into life, take on a new challenge and value your beautiful, extraordinary, enchanting, creative feminine authenticity. You are Yogini.

How to do it: Stand on your mat with feet approximately four feet apart. Turn your toes towards the corners of your mat and bend your knees. Make sure that your knees are going in the same direction as your toes. Stretch your arms out from your shoulders bend your elbows with fingers reaching up towards the sky. Take a deep breath in and as you exhale spread your fingers shooting positive, loving, feminine energy out from your fingertips into the world.

*I*n 2009 at the Vancouver Peace Summit, the Dali Lama made a profound statement that the Western woman will save the world. I take this very seriously that it is our responsibility to heal our families and so we can take our healed selves out into our communities and help others be the best that they can be. Value your feminine gifts that nurture our children to bring beauty and love into our homes. Leave behind any fears that others may be judging you, fiercely be yourself so that you will inspire others to do the same. For every group of people who may be judging us, all we need is one person to be inspired to step into their purpose.

When I went to India I saw oppression very clearly, it was extremely blatant. Oppression not only of the girls who were rescued out of brothels and safely in organizations where they were getting help and support, but the entire female population of the country are oppressed. Living in fear to walk the streets alone or take public transportation. What has developed upon returning home to Canada is how clearly I see oppression in my own home and community. I see where we women need to voice and reclaim our worth, and that our value doesn't get measured by a paycheck. I feel that once we claim our status for ourselves, then the rest of our population will recognize it as well.

As I write the statement, "I am Yogini" I feel proud and filled with emotions of awe. The emotions come as I imagine the millions of Yogini's, Goddesses and powerful women who have walked on this earth before us. I reflect on all of the women of the past centuries that have been horribly oppressed, denied and used, who remained strong and capable to adapt. When I reflect on oppression of women and girls in our world now, who are denied empowerment, I am saddened and appalled. Women have had to live lives that didn't feed their soul and devoid of opportunities for centuries. Yet through hardship women continue to rise up in the face of life threatening adversities. The history of women fascinates me.

Let's contemplate our connection, our insight and our growth due to Saints, Yogini's and Goddesses of our past:

Christian Goddesses: Mother Mary, Mary Magdalene, Saint Sophia, Joan of Arc and Mother Theresa.

Roman Goddesses: Fortuna, Venus, Diana, Athena and Flora.

Goddesses from Greece: Aphrodite, Psyche, Artemis, Hera, Demeter and Medusa.

Hindu Goddesses: Durga, Shakti, Kali, Lakshmi, Saraswati and Bhuvaneshwari.

Egyptian Goddesses: Isis, Hathor and Bast.

Many other Goddesses from cultures and belief systems including Tibet, Celtic, Middle East, Chinese, Welsh and Aboriginal have a similarity in honoring The Mother, Earth, Wisdom, Courage, Fertility, Beauty, Creativity and Love.

As we remember, I feel proud that Goddesses from the ancient times of Greece, India, and Rome are still being revered and worshiped while I find it amusing that the Goddesses of our time are called celebrities. These women are being adored, loved and recognized. Many of our modern day Goddesses – Oprah, Angelina Jolie, Taylor Swift, Meryl Streep, Ashley Judd, Sandra Bullock, Scarlett Johansson, Mille Cyrus, Kristen Stewart and others, help women and people all over the world. These women use their influence and resources to create change and achieving much as they follow their purpose in a strong connection to spirit. Let's also cheer the millions of unsung heroines! I am humbled to acknowledge that there have always been women of strength in all of our societies. Let's honor all women, reclaiming Yogini in our own right.

I am blessed to feel Goddess energy and to see Divine light in the many women whom I associate with. I love the feminine and I want all women to embrace their goddess, hold close that you are here to be the voice for peace, beauty and nurturing. Accept your fire and generate as you take back your body to embrace what you have been graced with.

It is in all types of careers where we can do great work, be our authentic selves and be an example for everyone around us. People will naturally be drawn to your calmness, to the light that you are shining and they will want that for themselves. You don't need to do anything except value and embody the person you were meant to be, the person you came here to be.

We are moving into a time and space where I believe if every woman takes a few minutes each day to connect to her Goddess energy, acknowledging her importance and worth, we can be a formidable community of cherished women and honored for the Yogini's that we are. What a world we are creating of the Divine Feminine who fight for their beliefs, who embrace their warrior spirit and who move gracefully through it all.

14
ARDHA CHANDRASANA – Half Moon

Perception, Harmony

*A*rdha **Chandrasana** is an opening posture where you maintain strength and balance. Half Moon pose wants you to look at things in your life from a different perspective. Is there a situation, question or problem you are struggling with? What if you changed your perception, even slightly, to give you a whole new understanding? Open up your heart, look honestly at what is happening and come from a different angle. Be receptive to new ideas, how to be supported and surrender. With a small modulation you can create harmonious and loving results.

How to do it: Stand at the front of your mat. Slightly bend right knee, place right hand on the floor or block about twelve inches in front of your foot. Gently extend left leg out behind you (parallel with the floor) as you straighten your right leg. Extend your left arm to the sky; bring your gaze forward opening your hips and chest.

*E*very person we have an interaction with is an integral part of our life journey. We have a sacred contract with most people that we encounter. He or she provides us with a chance for connection, a lesson or an experience to participate in. It is a wonderful thing when you think about the agreement that you have made with every person in every day. Each encounter gives us a chance to be authentic and open to opportunities.

When we meet a person or step into a new situation we get to decide our reaction. We can be unengaged, annoyed or judgmental; alternately we can engage, be loving, joyful and accepting. When we are aware and take responsibility for how we show up, we can shift our perspective and ultimately shift the energy for others as well.

How you move through this world and how you give to others is your choice, but be conscious that your behavior has a ripple effect and will affect more than just the person in front of you. Imagine the person standing in front of you is being rude to the cashier at the grocery store, it upsets her and then she in turn is rude to the next five customers that come through her till. One of those customers gets aggravated and drives off mad through the parking lot, a boy on a bike tries to spin out of the way and falls off his bike...on and on it goes.

We can come up with scenario after scenario. This is how connection works. We are all connected, we all have a soul and that soul has made contracts with other souls. Each soul desires the same things in life, to feel love, connection and worthiness. I've had several experiences in my life where the contract was extremely clear and precise.

It's an incredible idea to think that every encounter that we have with every person is a contract, a spiritual agreement that is here for our benefit. Before we come here into this physical body we have decided what experiences we are going to have and what lessons we are going to go through. We have scheduled who will be in our lives and what the union is.

This connection begins with you choosing your parents and siblings; the house where you will live and grow-up in, to the person you'll marry or not marry, the children you may or may not have, is all predetermined before you come here. You know on an energetic level when you meet someone that you have a strong connection with. It may be a love connection or it may be a hate connection but there are people that you instantly have a reaction to. Why? You may have known that person in a past life. You have an agreement or contract with them that you need to play out in this lifetime.

A very clear contract showed up when I was working as a grocery store cashier in high school. One particular incident I said "Merry Christmas!" to a gentleman in a happy joyful voice. He snarled at me and said he was Jewish and not everyone celebrates Christmas. I was shocked and taken off guard. Not because he didn't celebrate Christmas, but by how harsh he had reprimanded me. That exchange was a very specific sacred contract that we had and probably has influenced me more that he could ever imagine.

Let's remember that we are all connected and the littlest of comments, looks or gestures can influence another and perhaps many, many people all around the world. I don't think I have said Merry Christmas to a random person since that moment. I do not feel incensed or resentful for that fact, I feel it has put me in a more aware position where I respect all religions and have no desire to push any religion on anyone. Though I do not consider myself a Christian, I am extremely spiritual and I enjoy celebrations and traditions. I observe some of the Christian traditions because they are the customs of my childhood. I also have added over the years traditions from other cultures and faiths into my life. I observe the New and Full Moons; I monitor both solstices and equinoxes, including celebrating with a winter solstice party. Travelling and experiencing other cultures continues to open my soul to new ideas and opportunities.

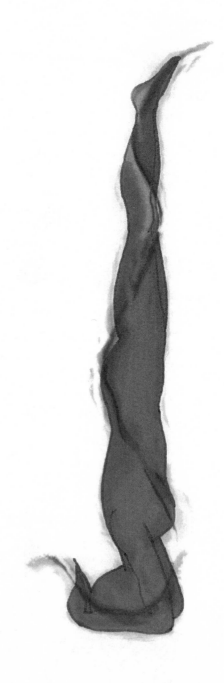

15

SIRSASANA - Head Stand

King, Challenge

S irsasana is the King of yoga postures and is telling you to push your limits. Head Stand wants you to step out of your comfort zone and move with confidence towards your goals. Rejoice in mastering a great challenge. If you have been thinking about taking on a new venture now is the time to do so. Is today the day that you jump out of a plane? Color your hair red? Or stand on your head? If not now, when? If not you, then who? This card wants you to tap into your masculine, powerful, risk taking energy. Revel in the feeling of empowerment, confidence and drive. Then feel the excitement of a challenge.

How to do it: Place your elbows on the mat, shoulder width apart, lace your fingers together. Place the top of your head on the floor with your hands cradling your head, press your elbows into the mat, engaging your shoulders to lift your head slightly off the mat and no longer on the floor. Walk your toes towards your nose. Draw your knees into your chest and when ready extend your legs towards the sky. Wow!

$\mathcal{M}$y first thought when I became aware of Off the Mat, Into the World's™, Global Seva Challenge to raise $20,000.00 for victims of sex trafficking in India was "Yes, I need to do this!!!" I knew instantly that I was called to do this challenge and that it was time for me to take off my rose-colored glasses and step up. I knew I was meant to help all those little girls, young women and some boys. That was my first thought!

My second thought was "How on earth am I ever going to raise that kind of money? I'm not a fund-raiser so how am I going to be able to do that?" I took a week to meditate on it, look for and receive signs to help me make a decision that my soul had already made. I could see that this decision would impact my life, my family and my business but I wasn't sure how and if I should be doing it. I thought about what other people would think and I thought about the impact of bringing this type of information into my home, psyche and body.

Eventually I heard myself say to a friend. "I don't want to be on my death bed and say, "You know, I wish I had at least tried to raise that money for girls in India." When I heard those words spilling out of my mouth they stuck with me. That's when I sent in my commitment, I was going to do the Global Seva Challenge-India!

Instantly hearing the calling to do this work and know I was meant to help. I also knew that even if I didn't achieve the goal, whatever monies I did raise, would make a huge impact on their lives. I also knew that I was given an opportunity to fulfill my strong lifelong desire to make a difference. So, I jumped in with both feet.

What happened was life changing for me and this book is not specifically written for me to talk about this important cause (please read Half the Sky: Turning Oppression into Opportunity for Women Worldwide by Nicholas D. Kristof and Sheryl WuDunn). In fact, I don't think I would have written this book if...NO, let me clarify, I would not have written this book if I hadn't taken the risk and made the leap of faith to do the Global Seva Challenge.

Once I decided to take the daunting project on to raise money, the first thing I did was to reach out to my friends and community and ask if anyone would be willing to help me for one year. I sent emails to the people who had taken our Yoga In Action Training Workshops and asked if anyone would like to be on my Dream Team to help me with fund raising. Remarkably I got eight of the most beautiful, strong and amazing women to help me and so the Dream Team was formed. I also received additional support for products to sell and administrative help. The women and men in my life were invaluable.

Together our Dream Team met bi-weekly so we could brain storm, plan and figure out some really great ways of how we could raise that kind of money. It began with doing karmic yoga in my studio every Sunday morning taught by fellow yoga teachers from around the city. I had a screening of the *Yogawoman* movie in my studio. It was a successful evening, plus it started to get the word out that I was doing fund raising, getting attention from people who were interested in yoga and the cause. The yoga community of Grande Prairie, Alberta, Canada was amazing, supportive and a huge help. They all came together with little egos and big hearts.

Next I reached out to the Indian community and "An Evening at the Taj" was developed. Our Dream Team gathered silent auction items for us to sell and we sold out of tickets quickly. Again the event was a huge success.

Extending out to the incredibly supportive yoga community I organized a Yoga Conference with top instructors volunteering their time to teach workshops. This was such a gift to our community where participants could be exposed to all types of yoga, teachers and philosophies.

In nine months I had reached the goal of raising $20,000.00 and I was then able to go to India in the New Year. This was such a great feeling of living in the flow of life completely on purpose. I conquered the challenge and completed what I set out to do. Feeling thrilled and amazed with how the universe and the Divine helped me through this process. I was proud of what I had accomplished and filled with gratitude for tremendous encouragement, support and help from my Dream Team, family and community.

> **If not you, Who? If not now, When?**

16

VAPARITA KARINI - Legs up the wall

Nurturing, Healing

Vaparita **Karini** posture is the chicken soup of yoga. When you are feeling down, in any way, this posture will help. Legs Up the Wall is for nurturing yourself with love and kindness. Here you reverse the flow, quiet the mind and refresh your heart and lungs. Have you been under the weather lately? Tired, stressed, but don't know why? This is the time to have a "sick" day. When we continue to burn the candle at both ends for weeks, our body will eventually shut us down. This is your free pass, take a day and only do what is absolutely necessary. Stay in bed and watch old movies, read a book, drink tea and eat dark chocolate and nuts. Do this each month on the first day of your period or on the full moon. Enjoy feeling the nurturing, healing love.

How to do it: Lie on the floor with your buttocks close to the wall, swing your legs up the wall. With your back on your mat, your legs up a wall, relax with your eyes closed, place your arms down by your sides and restore.

We live in a society where we work extremely hard. There is an expectation in North America that you will work long hours, take little time off and that is how you will become successful. We take very few days off and often give up our evenings and weekends to work. Even when we are doing what we love, we can find ourselves feeling overworked, overwhelmed and burnt out.

Eventually our body will shut us down. We will get sick so that we are forced to take several days off. I encourage you to do that before your body makes you. When things are getting too much, take some days to look after yourself and your body. Just a little bit extra sleep can make a huge impact. You will be able to cope better, feel more in control of your emotions and won't need to go to other stimuli to jazz you up. Your body and mind will function optimally.

There have been times in my life, years in fact, where I was unhappy and stressed to think about my next day, dreaded thinking about having to get up in the morning. I didn't want to be doing what I did or at least what I thought I had to do each day. I got angry a lot and I would have freak-outs and yell. Other times I was crying in the shower and wondering how I was going to get out of this situation. I kept asking the question, "How can I make this better? How can I gain control?"

It was a slow and steady process of reading lots of books, talking to friends and spiritual workers, taking workshops, and exercising. With many, many baby steps I finally came to a place where I was content on Sunday night. I wasn't freaking out as often, I noticed that I hadn't cried in months and I felt more in control and able to look after myself. I was no longer crabby and having bad days.

Then as the years went along I realized that I was constantly in a state of gratitude for my life. I was happy and I loved what I did each day; I had great relationships and was able to exclaim "I LOVE MY LIFE!" Now if I start to get crabby, I am able to give myself what I need. Maybe it's a nap; sometimes I'll invite friends over for some laughs. I feel better after a good workout or an extra inspiring yoga practice.

For years now, I live and study yoga almost every day. Remembering when I step off my mat that it is okay to live a lifestyle of simplicity but also with purpose. With the yoga lifestyle and making conscious decisions we are able to honor when our body needs to rest or alternately, power up.

Are you able to stay balanced when things get "crazy-busy"? Can you remain in your core and find what you need to do to maintain your optimal health to allow for sustainability? The first thing that I do when I am feeling overwhelmed or like life is taking over on me is get more sleep. Honestly it is as simple as that. When we are rested we are more able to cope with our life and the demands that are put on us. Plus it gives us the strength to do what we have committed to for our wellness.

How to create sustainability is by living in a way that will support you and your efforts physically, mentally and spiritually.

Sustainability Practice:

1. **Diet**
   Eat healthy, light meals. I am vegetarian and I have been since I was 16 years old. However, protein is extremely important to regulate blood sugar. As a vegetarian, I make sure that I get some protein at each meal. Whether you eat meat or not, make your meals light with lots of fresh vegetables, fruit and Whole grains. Clean fresh water and lean protein.

2. **Rest**
   Sleep is the number one best way to bring us back into balance and into being able to handle life. I know when I have been having a lot of late nights, or early mornings I start to get touchy and unable to cope and suspect that I might be getting sick. Sleep is key to getting healthy again. Try to add an extra half hour of sleep each night to your routine.

3. **Exercise**

   Exercise and move your body every day. I start each morning off with a yoga breathing and asana practice. Every day is different but by adding some form of practice it will bring you into consciousness to connect with your inner self. Then, participate in other exercise throughout the day to burn off steam, sweat out toxins and release endorphins. I like to walk, run, go on the elliptical or get outside.

4. **Breathing**

   I know, I know, it sounds ridiculous that we need to schedule in breathing. But honestly, taking a deep breath is the easiest and most perfect way of calming us down. It relaxes our central nervous system and brings us back into the present moment. Our breath can get so shallow at times, so add long, smooth, deep breaths. Add Durga Pranayama (Chapter 44) when you want to slow down and de-stress.

5. **Meditation**

   Meditation for me is a non-negotiable. I must meditate every day to maintain my health, wellbeing and sustainability. Meditation is as essential as eating, when I don't eat I get irritable and if I don't meditate I get agitated. Meditate in the morning, in the afternoon, or in the evening at least once each day. It creates calm that you'll feel spread throughout your entire household. Your meditation can be mantra meditation, walking in nature, looking at an item or following your breath. Find some time each day in quiet and in silence for meditation.

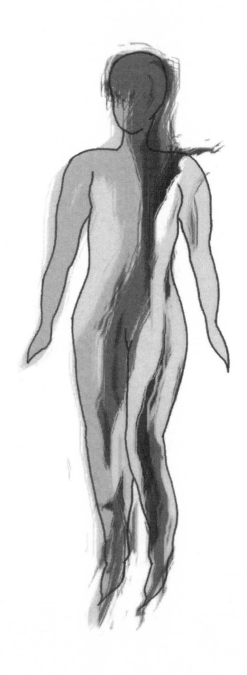

17

TADASANA - Mountain

Balance, Stabilized

*T*adasana is a grounding posture that balances both sides of our body. In Mountain pose we stand steady and stable. How balanced is your life between finances, family, relationships, wellness, career and creativity? Which area of your life is taking the forefront? What part is virtually non-existent? Life can always get out of balance, but when we stay grounded and find our stability, we can cope with poise. Take this opportunity to drop into your body, press your feet into the floor, breathe deeply, and be present. Take a look around, and notice that at this moment you are safe. Say an affirmation, "I am safe and stable." "I create a life of harmony and balance." These techniques generate mental steadiness, emotional stability and a habit of calm behavior to rise to life's imbalances.

How to do it: Stand on your mat with your big toes touching, heels slightly parted, weight spread evenly throughout the feet. Legs are strong, pull-up your pelvic floor and tighten your abdominal muscles. Slide your shoulders down your back with your arms at your sides. Chin is parallel to the floor with your gaze straight ahead.

*W*here does your life seem most out of balance, or consumes most of your time and energy? Which area takes up so much energy that you are struggling to catch your breath or it feels like you are walking sideways? Does it feel like you are swimming upstream and the current keeps pulling you back down the river? This is how it feels when we live off purpose and when certain areas take over.

Take a moment to check in to notice how balanced your life feels right now. Where is most of your time and energy going?

Family/Home life:
Social/Relationships:
Work/School:
Finances:
Exercise/Diet:
Rest:
Meditation:
Creativity:

From the above categories, which area is almost non-existent, where little of your energy gets distributed? When we live for long periods of time out of balance, it can take even longer to stabilize. We can't avoid getting out of sync from time to time, life gets disrupted and some of those changes create imbalance. However, when we can't catch our breath and it goes on for too long it becomes detrimental to our health and wellbeing.

To come back into balance we first need to look at which area of our life is taking over and which area of our life is getting absolutely no airtime. Usually the first thing to go is our creativity. We get beat down with all that we have to do and we don't think creativity is important. As part of our makeup, we humans need to have a sense of creativity in our lives. Take a look at how you can increase your creativity or take a look at what you are already doing and add flair to it.

I don't know about you but there have times that it is 6:30 p.m. and I need to get some food made for my family. I have had to get extremely creative to produce something out of what I have in my refrigerator and my cupboards. In fact at times I have thought, here is the true Witch in me that can conjure up this meal out of virtually thin air.

I find my creativity when I design brochures and flyers for advertising, blogging or updating my web site. I get inspired and use my creativity to build a beautiful flow yoga class or an inspiring workshop. I might start moving furniture around at midnight and last winter I started knitting dishcloths (well I made one). I cherish family and travel photos and will print a bunch off some days, and my friend Heather makes me music playlists. Where are you adding your creative essence into your life?

The next thing that gets out of balance is our relationships. We don't find the time to see our friends. Spending time with other women, couples and your best friend will feed your soul. Socializing with people who love you, laughing and sharing inside jokes or finding joy in recounting stories will make our lives more meaningful and fulfill the connection that our soul needs.

Then we stop our self-care practice of eating healthy, exercising and resting. We put ourselves on the back burner. When we're super busy, that is the precise time we need to slow down and look after ourselves. If we're out of balance illness shows up and we are forced to take some time to heal.

It's true that finding balance can be a challenge. Take small steps to first recognize where you are putting most of your energy and strive to add beneficial practices that will allow you to gain balance and stability.

18

KAPOTASANA - Pigeon

Emotion, Feeling

*K*apotasana posture will open your hips to emotions, feelings and sensation. Pigeon is a supportive and rewarding posture that allows you to stay with the sensations in your body and breathe deeper. Recognize and acknowledge your feelings without trying to change or control them. When we suppress, what we deem as negative feelings, then we also suppress our positive emotions. Know that all feelings are fleeting and will not last. Follow sensation as it moves through the body, perhaps going from heart to belly to throat or shoulders. What memories, thoughts or words might go along with this awareness? Now is the time to pound a pillow, have a big cry, talk with a friend or write a letter. Release anger and sadness, disappointment and fear. Sit with the emotion for a bit and then surround yourself with positive energy that will uplift your spirits as you return to your true self. Repeat your affirmation. "I love and accept myself."

How to do it: Start on your hands and knees. Bring your right knee to the front of your mat, and extend your left leg out the back of your mat. Place your hands on either side of your front knee. If you are able (while maintaining hips squared to the front of the mat) bring your right foot towards your left hand. Raise your heart center towards the sky, and then slowly lower your forehead to the floor (option stack hands to place forehead on hands). Repeat with the other leg.

E motions, feeling and sensation - how do they show up in our lives and what do they create? Let's recognize that every emotion we have is very real. They are real for our partners, spouses, children, friends and us. The next point to notice about our emotions is that they don't last very long. They come and then they go and it is how we react to those emotions that make the difference for us. When we let our anger turn into rage or turn into days of a bad mood then we need to look at that. We are no longer angry because the emotion of anger only lasts a mere two minutes and then it dissipates.

Our response to an attack will be fight, flight or freeze. When we freeze, we hold all the emotions in our body and it will create dis ease. Dis ease can show up as pain or discomfort and eventually illness.

It is extremely important to not suppress emotions. When we get triggered or when confronted, it creates restrictions in our body. What does it look like when we suppress our emotions? When we suppress our emotions we put ourselves into a freeze state. We are not moving or moving very little, we are freaking on the inside yet pretending everything is okay on the outside. As the emotion dissipates then we can again move freely, but in the mean time what has happened to that emotion in our body? It will create restriction. Some part of our body will hold it.

Take a moment to think about this. We are in a conversation and someone says something that angers or shames you, the comment comes straight out of left field and you stop in your tracks. You decidedly do not want your anger to erupt, so you stop! You freeze as you flip through the appropriate responses in your head. Nothing comes to you, you don't know what to say to this comment, so you say and do nothing. You can feel the heat rise, your breathing quickens and perhaps your jaw clenches or shoulders tighten. A heat spreads through your body. You may even feel self-conscious about trying to take a deep relaxing breath, or as you try to take a deep breath it catches in your chest. Other people may even be watching you to gauge your reaction. The conversation carries on and you think you are over it. You think the person is an idiot who knows nothing about you and what you are doing. You may even find yourself complaining to a friend about what a jerk he is.

You have suppressed the feelings into your body. You know that your body had several physical reactions to the confrontation, so now what happens to it? If you find yourself thinking about it again at a later date, it has landed. As you repeat the comment in your mind, notice where you are feeling it in your body. This is another perfect example of the mind/body connection. Wherever you are feeling it is where you have created the restriction. You might find a twinge in your stomach, in your back, in your shoulders, eyes or your chest. You may feel something in your knees, hips or neck. Perhaps you find your jaw is tightening or your hands are clenching. Once you notice where the sensation is, just stay in that area and ask yourself "what was it about the comment, why is it showing up in that place?" It will probably bring up a deeper reason; a memory, a thought or a word will come to you. Talk it through with your spiritual director, therapist or counselor. Release it from your body through your yoga practice and tap into affirmations to counter the negative comments. Always come back to the affirmation, "I love and accept myself". If we don't catch these times when we suppress our emotions they will continue to expand and grow until they create limiting beliefs, dis ease and illness.

Now, I'm not saying that we want to go crazy and become aggressive, inappropriate or wearing our emotions on our sleeve acting out every feeling and sensation. When we go into fight response, we feel out of control or lost and we end up feeling much worse after things calm down. However, we do need to address the emotions when they come up. It's a good opportunity to ask "why am I being triggered, what lesson is here for me and where am I holding it in my body?" It is significant for us to think about why are we feeling the way we are feeling and is it truth? Is it me, or am I being triggered by something?

See if you can use your body as a gauge. I have been given pain and discomfort into various areas of my body that I recognize instantly when they pop up as something to be aware of. Every twinge is an indicator that I am falling back into old patterns and beliefs that are no longer serving me.

When I get a lower backache, I KNOW that I am not being authentic. My pain tells me that I have fallen back into patterns that I don't like, I feel bad or ashamed of. What I do is instantly start reaffirming, "I love and accept myself." Then not only do I release the pattern but I also release the annoyance I have for myself to have fallen back into that pattern. Here is a very clear example.

I do not like the pattern I have of going into a place of negativity. I don't like myself when I complain about other people and what they are doing.

Several years ago when my son was playing hockey, I took him to another city for a weekend hockey tournament. My husband was unable to attend the event so my oldest son, Forrester came with my youngest hockey player, Jenkins and myself. As sometimes happen at these types of sporting events, parents get annoyed with referees and the opposing teams. We attended the first game on Friday evening and then two more games on Saturday. By Saturday afternoon I was agreeing with the other parents of how unfair the refereeing was and the injustice of it all. By Saturday night every time I rolled over in bed, my lower back would scream at me. I instantly tapped into the affirmation "I love and accept myself, I love and accept myself, I love and accept myself." By Sunday morning my back was healed. Before the Sunday game was over I had to leave the arena and wait in the car. The flight response was my best option in this circumstance. I could no longer remain healthy and in my core while I was in that environment. I hated what was going on in my head and what I wanted to yell out along with the crowd.

I know without a shadow of a doubt that the backache was a direct result of how I went into a place and began to act in a way that does not align with my beliefs. Others might think my back hurt from sitting in a cold arena, driving to the tournament and sleeping in a hotel bed. I want to reiterate that I know that my back hurt not because I was in a negative energy, it hurt because I was joining the negative energy and I don't like that about myself. I was joining in, in the blame. Not verbally, but I was agreeing in my head and energetically I was adding to the negative, ridiculous and volatile energy. It felt like an out of body experience had taken over me making me feel horrible. I was on edge and disconnected with the bigger picture.

19

CHATARANGA DANDASANA - Plank

Strength, Capabilities

*C*hataranga Dandasana is a strong posture where you tap into your mental state and ask, "Can I do this?" The answer is a resounding "YES!" You have got this; life is going well because you are strong and capable. Plank reminds you that you can't quit. Your ambitions and dreams are worth it! Notice what's holding you back and creating limitations in your life. Are you getting in your own way? When we make conscious decisions, add a change or create something new, we are often met with resistance. Resistance asks you "how much do you want this? How will you keep moving towards your goal?" Have you been keeping yourself from your full potential? Do you dim your light to make others feel more comfortable? Now is the time to expand yourself, use your strength and your ability. You can do it, so go big!

How to do it: On your mat, start on your hands and knees. Extend your feet out behind you and lift onto your hands and toes. To modify for any shoulder or back discomfort, please lower your knees and/or elbows onto the mat. Engage your core and breathe into your diaphragm.

When we put ourselves out there taking risks, we are opening ourselves up for criticism. Others may not want to do what we are doing; yet they may still criticize and judge. How do we handle it? How do we react? Sometimes we want to quit. We think it might be best to stop what we believe in, even to the point where we get in the way of our accomplishments. We question ourselves as to what we are doing; we ask "who do we think we are" and generate sabotage. Ideally we stay strong and determined with our capabilities and avoid the negative energy.

I got a very strong sensation to shut myself down immediately after participating in a Ladies in Red, Heart and Stroke Fundraising Event. I wasn't keen on doing it, which is a pattern of resistance that shows up in my life. If I was asked to go on stage and be seen or public speak, I would shy away from it. I rationalized that I didn't really need any new business and someone else could do it.

Here is the twist this time, I was told that the idea to do this had come directly out of one of my yoga classes and the people organizing the event told me, if I couldn't do it this year they would wait and I could do it next year. What? When I realized that I wasn't ever going to get out of it, I took a deep breath and said, "OK, I can do it."

Once the decision was made, then I really wanted to make sure it was going to be good. I choreographed a small yoga display and wrote out a short yoga presentation. The organizers invited two other instructors from other studios for us to do it together. On the evening of the event the room was packed. There were a lot of people in the audience whom I knew and for me, it was a big deal.

This is a sellout event every year, as the prominent women from my community pour into the event dressed in red to watch a fashion show, mingle with friends and acquaintances and support the cause. The food and décor is glorious, the energy is festive and classy. Let's just say it; I really did not want to make a fool of myself! I was nervous and unsure of what on earth was I doing. I was chatting to a really good friend of mine and I said to her: "What am I doing this for? I don't need the extra business, this is ridiculous!" She calmly said to me, "Well it's not really about you, it's about women in this room with heart disease and they need to be doing yoga." Wham! Wow, was she right! I needed to get out of my own way. We flowed through our demonstration of heart opening yoga postures and embodied the importance of maintaining good physical health for our hearts. The event went well, we gave our presentation flawlessly and I enjoyed the remainder of the evening.

This statement "It's not about you, it's about you doing this to benefit and help other people." has helped me many more times since that day. It is a statement that I tell myself when I am nervous and stressed out about giving a talk about the girls I met in India, about the victims of sex trafficking or about health and wellness. I remind myself that it's not about me, I am the vessel from spirit and I am here to bring the message to people listening.

The very next morning I was taking something out to the garage, and I noticed that the door was locked. This was unusual since we only locked that inside door at night. By this time of morning there had already been family coming and going. I went out to the garage thinking that was odd; I decided when I came back in I would re-lock the door. I didn't know why, but I felt drawn to do so.

Just then my cell phone rang. I was in a great, positive mood after doing the presentation the night before and I felt it had turned out well. I had spent time with friends and other women in my community and I felt very connected, and happy to have been seen. When I picked up my cell phone I saw that it was a blocked call. I had a split second of doubt, which was a very clear intuitive hit that this wasn't right. My body instantly started vibrating and I was swept with an ominous feeling. The man on the line asked for me by name and then started to ask me questions about yoga. He mentioned his wife and his daughters. I was still unsure and on guard, the phone call died and then he called back immediately, saying that he got cut off. I continued to answer his questions, as they got progressively inappropriate. I was just about done with this, when boom he was off the phone.

The shakes and sensations were already happening and the energy was moving swiftly through my body. My very first thought was "Oh shit, I shouldn't have been on that stage last night, I won't do that again. I can't be seen!" Luckily, my second thought was "fuck that!" Here was the resistance that could have shut me down, but I wouldn't let it! I don't believe that this person lives in my community or even was at the Red Dress Event. I believe that it was pure and simple resistance that was showing up in my life, that the universe orchestrated on my behalf to challenge me. It was an opportunity to ask myself again, "How badly do I want to live on purpose, get my message across and serve my highest aspiration?"

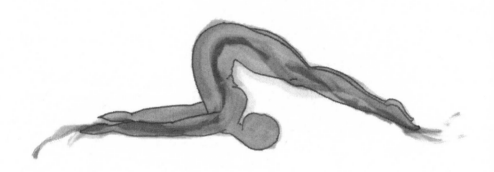

20

HALASANA - Plow

Slow, Steady

*H*alasana posture gives an incredible stretch yet allows you to stay safely on the ground. Plow is a somewhat awkward position that isn't always pretty. This card tells you, that you are at the point of just breaking through the surface. This is the time to set the groundwork for new beginnings and to keep plugging away at your project. Have obstacles come up? Do you go around? Do you go through? Change direction? Or do you remove the barrier? So often we are looking for the big tada, and when things become mundane we lose interest. Remain with the slow and steady progression, all the while envisioning what you want to create as the bigger picture. Stay open and receptive to new ideas and visions. Life is not always exciting but you are breaking ground and preparing to plant the seeds, notice the perfection of nature and the magic in the everyday.

How to do it: Lie on your back and lift your heels to the sky. Roll your hips up off the floor and support your lower back with your palms. When ready lower your feet to the floor above your head. Breathe slowly and steadily.

$\mathcal{K}$ eep at it; continue working towards your projects and goals. This is where the belief that hard work pays off comes into play. Though this may be a limiting belief, sometimes we get to a point where we have to put our nose to the ground and get some of our tasks done. You know that you are the sole creator of your life; though beliefs, timing and our own fear can prevent us from taking the steps in making it all unfold without doubt. Every day take a step forward on your dream by doing one task that will benefit your goal. Feel grateful for what you have already done by celebrating the achievements. Notice what slows you down or deters you from progress.

I remember someone once said, "My ego is trying to kill me!" At the time that struck me as very funny, but you know, sometimes it feels that way! It feels like we aren't going fast or big enough. Some days I'm going along and everything is great and then bam, I get hit with doubt. I could be working harder, smarter, be more successful or making more money. Aha! "Hello Ego". It is vital for us to recognize when our ego shows and strikes at our self-esteem. We can stop our ego in its tracks and recognize that we are good enough. We are amazing just the way we are. Feel good with what we are doing without putting so much pressure on ourselves and enjoy life. There have been days when my self-esteem feels very low and I feel that people aren't happy with what I am doing or how I am running my business. I have never been comfortable with confrontation and I would prefer if everyone was just happy and loved me. Wouldn't we all? That's when we can remind ourselves to not take things personally. "Q-tip" – Quit Taking It Personally. Take it slow, learn the skills that are needed and create from the ground up.

When we get a desire to take a course or start towards a new goal we are planting seeds for a greater picture. We go step by step towards the dream. Then as we close in on the dream more seeds get planted that will keep us excited and motivated. We talk to a person, read a book or get an email that makes us sit up and take notice. We think and ponder the idea until we move towards it. This is how life works as we move through the stages of starting, growing, expanding and ending, soon to start again. We become discontent when we hold on to the illusion of security and sometimes we may resist leaving our comfort zone. Acknowledge those periods where we make slow and steady progress towards our goals and notice the importance of all the work that gets done.

My own personal ego guides me to feel pressured or responsible to please others, to feel like I'm not good enough and that there is something wrong with me. With that then came a feeling of disconnection and giving up my authenticity. My head would take me to a place where I wanted to shut down. I wanted to shut myself off and escape into the dreary of the ordinary, to a place that wasn't my authentic self. I felt a need for disconnection and I wondered why bother? All of these feelings are ego. Ego wants me to resist shining my light. Remind yourself that what you're doing is good enough and work steadily with confidence.

21

PARSVOTTONASANA - Pyramid

Ancient, Cellular Memory

*P*arsvottonasana is a yoga posture that requires stability and provides an intense stretch. As you step into Pyramid, stay solid in your grounding, when stuck relax, breathe deeply and move forward on the exhalation. Have you ever asked yourself, "How do I know that?" "Where did I learn this?" Somehow you just "get it". When you do anything for the first time and it feels like you've done this before. Something that you're naturally good at, you find easy and you notice that this is what you have always been drawn to. This is our cellular memory; it may have come through ancestors, or previous lifetimes. Celebrate this talent that is unique to you, embrace it and continue to breathe as you move forward. Cherish, value, and embrace this pure unique talent that has been gifted to you.

How to do it: Stand at the front of your mat, step your left foot back. Keep your hips squared to the front of your mat. With your hands in prayer mudra behind your back, slowly exhale and extend over your front leg. If available place your hands on the floor.

When I was a little girl I would get knowingness about certain things. I didn't know how I knew them or who had taught it to me but I would know things to be true. Feeling there was something more out there I wondered who was communicating with me. I always felt that I was here to do something really important for the world. If you feel this way, or if there was a period of time when you have felt that way, then you know exactly what I am talking about. You know that you are here to do something amazing and somehow along the years life has gotten in the way. Now you want to live a life full of purpose, full of consciousness, joy and pleasure. I believe most of us feel this way and have a strong desire to explore and expand our potential.

Things are not happening TO you, they are just happening and you are here to go through them. Can you imagine how boring life would be if we just went along and nothing ever changed? Our soul would stop expanding and we would stay in a reactionary level without movement and growth. Can you imagine that kind of life? I know that because you are reading this book that you want to continue to explore and do your own personal inner work.

I had a client once who is a very talented and gifted painter. As she continued to paint and expanded her exposure, her paintings were increasing in value. She came to me and wondered what were these people thinking? Why did they find her artwork so great that they would pay that kind of money for them? She said her paintings were so easy and simplistic that anyone could do it. She honestly did not get it. She felt like a fraud and in fact no longer wanted to keep painting. This extremely talented artist was suffering from a belief that she needed to be a struggling artist. She didn't value her beautiful astounding ancient and spiritual gifts. Since her talent came so easily to her, she didn't think it was worth much. I worked with her on self worth and reminded her that this is a unique gift that had been bestowed on her. No others in this entire universe had this exact same gift and so, by not fulfilling this gift she would do the world a disservice.

Recognize your gifts. They are different for each one of us. Even though there are thousands and thousands of yoga instructors, millions of hair stylists, an abundance of restaurants, teachers, medical professionals and repair people, each and every person has a special gift that is unique to them. You are no different. Identify, embrace and value your significant expertise.

I started meditating at thirteen years old and I have always felt a strong connection to the spirit world, yet in my thirties came a time where I found myself searching for a deeper connection. I didn't know what to do, my youngest child Jenkins was a year old and I knew that it was time for me move into something that would feed my soul.

I began with reading books on spirituality, Wiccan and mediums. I explored energy work, astrology and the elements. I was looking for a connection. I was desperate to spend time with women who would be interested in spirituality and spiritual growth, a chance for us to talk with and share our insight. I knew the feeling of what I was looking for, of meeting with other women to form regular connections, adding ritual and education. I could feel the benefits of being with other Goddesses, Yogini's and Diva's to share, talk through the cycles, support, encourage, challenge and transform.

It was during this time of searching, questioning and the strong desire to live my dharma, when I decided to become a yoga instructor. While I was in my daily meditation the message came very clearly to me. "Become a yoga instructor!" I had been pondering other alternatives at the time. Meditation instructor, life coach, hypnotherapy and wedding officiate. When the message to become a yoga instructor came, I knew instantly that this was my direction. This message came as clear and direct insight and I felt in my body a pure and resounding, "YES!"

When I took my training it came easy and fully. It felt like I had known this information for many lifetimes and I loved every aspect of yoga. I was in my mid thirties so was strong and confident in my yoga postures, yet I also loved the philosophy and gentleness of yoga. The diet and meditation practice had already been well established in me and I embraced chanting and breath work as second nature.

As clear as this message was, we also know that we cannot live fully on purpose without support from others. I spoke of my dream and desires to others and received insight and guidance to manifest my calling. When we can express what energies and directions we are contemplating with other goddesses, we get immeasurable reassurance and support. Remember to embrace new affirmations, "I move easily into new opportunities with ease and grace." "I advance into transformation and my feminine power with simplicity and love." I cherish the connection that I share with sisters and I believe that when we come together and spend time in relationship with a spiritual underlay we will flourish. When we do oracle cards, share insight, and talk about signs that come to us then we will move confidently following ancient cellular memory into spiritual abundance.

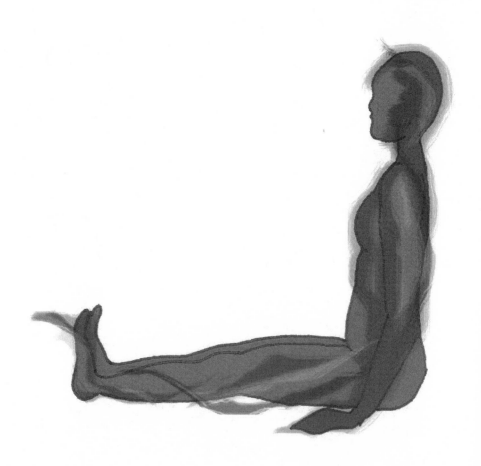

22

DANDASANA - Seated Staff

Individuality, Character

*D*andasana posture engages every muscle in our body. During Seated Staff pose you are solidly grounded and connected to the earth. An unwavering strength of character epitomizes the grounded soul. Can you maintain your position? Is there anything pulling or pushing you into something you don't want? This card is telling you to tap into your steadfast, emotionally dependable self. Instead of getting stuck in your vision, snap into action no matter what it takes. Find yourself getting more and more comfortable in being uncomfortable. Taking a risk doesn't mean you have all the answers, despite the discomfort make your decisions from what you want, instead of what you think others want. Relationships built with a stable foundation will flourish and endure. Start before you're ready!

How to do it: Sit on your mat with legs extended and engaged, toes drawn back towards shins. Slide your shoulders blades down your back; engage your core and press palms into the floor beside your hips. Chin is parallel with the floor. Gaze forward, breath steady.

*H*aving a strong sense of character is an ability to create your life and to not let society or someone else's ideas shake your confidence and drive. My definition of selfishness is when you don't do what someone else wants you to do. Are you being told that you are selfish because you are following your own path and working towards your goals? When our loved ones foundations start to tremble with some disruption there may be backlash. That is when you will need to stay connected to the earth and to your unshakeable knowing. Reassure them, but set your boundaries and express your own personal and professional needs without fear, guilt or shame.

This is the part of us that defines who we are. We can pretend to be something that we're not to the outside world but inside we know our truth. Observe how you may be holding yourself back from doing things that you would like to do. It takes a lot of strength of character to remain an individual and to keep moving towards your souls calling. There is a lot of courage and determination that you will need to have for this forward motion.

The journey of self-inquiry is often uncomfortable, not only for ourselves, but for the people who love us as well. They may want to protect you from experiencing the discomfort and keep you safe in their arms. Yet we yearn to stretch out and find some form of ease in the awkward. Only when we have truly looked at the uneasiness can we really get to know it.

We see strong characters when people are faced with adversity and remain determined in their conviction and their beliefs of what is truth. When I was in India I learnt that after the girls were rescued out of the brothel, they were put into a facility for three months to reverse the affects of "seasoning". "Seasoning" happens when they are first trafficked. The young girls are treated abominably to wipe out their confidence, their fire and to strip away their character. Fortunately, we know that the human soul and a person's individuality cannot be taken away. It stays intact even if we hide it from the outside world.

I myself found that I was trying to hide my spirituality. From the outside my life looked happy and beautiful yet on the inside I knew something was missing. Fear of ridicule, confrontation and an illusion of security kept me wanting to hide who I truly was. I was afraid to speak up and found myself laughing at things I thought were horrible. Many insightful and generous people recognized and appreciated what I was offering which encouraged me to show up more and more.

When I became a yoga instructor I knew that it was the perfect career path for me. I was able to talk about spirituality and wellness in a way that was socially acceptable. I begin my classes with offering a few minutes of education to promote good health and wellness, then breath work and an "Om" to connect us to our body and our spirit. Yoga offers us a way to show up on our mat that is unique and authentic to ourselves. In our yoga practice there is no judgment, other than from our own minds. We can get honest with ourselves and witness what is coming to the surface. Each day when we get on our mat we are connecting to the part of ourselves that wants to come out and be shared. We connect to our deep soul that wants to heal so our individual character can be exposed.

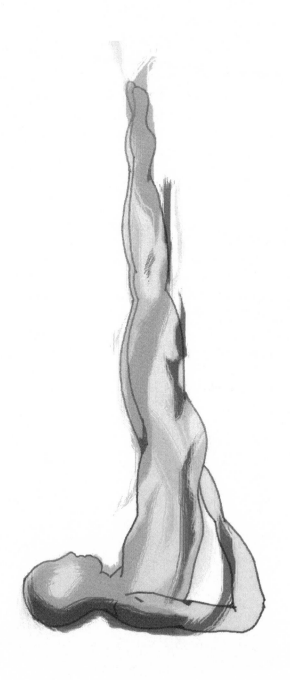

23

SARVANGASANA - Shoulder Stand

Queen, Empower

Sarvangasana is an inversion, which counteracts the effects of gravity. Shoulder Stand represents the Queen replete with knowledge and wisdom. Are you aware of how deserving you are? Can you acknowledge how blessed and beautiful the life that you have created is? Realize the bravery that you have to be open and empowered. When we can find the courage to ask for and take what we need, it shows strength of our authentic self. Now is the time to guide and show others as you lead by example. You are able to tell someone what happened and how it made you feel, now tell him or her what YOU need, and ask for it! Live the way you were meant to and lead with your loving heart. It takes confidence to command with compassion.

How to do it: Lie on your back and extend your feet to the sky. Lift your back off the mat to roll onto your shoulders. Support your lower back with your palms and gently tuck your elbows under. Soften your throat.

*T*o me an empowered woman is someone who has done and continues to do, deep soul searching to stay true to her life's purpose. She has gone into pursuit to live as fully as she can. Sometimes this means living a life rather different than the general population. She will have to question beliefs that may otherwise limit her fulfilling her true path. This might be looked upon as selfish behavior from an outsider, but is in fact extremely rewarding for herself, those closest around her and ultimately the entire world.

What are the qualities of an empowered woman?

- Someone who looks after herself and her wellbeing so as to create sustainability.
- Someone who consciously and conscientiously looks at what she is doing and why.
- She pauses before she speaks or commits.
- Someone who is serving the highest intention and questions how she can continue to serve others.
- She has the confidence, strength and compassion to step out of the norm, into and through the shadow, all for the sake of betterment.
- She lives on purpose and brings joy to herself that spreads out into her home, community and world.
- This woman takes full responsibility for all of her life's experiences. She has a strong connection to a higher power and a higher purpose, so will wait for the answers to come, knowing they will when they are suppose to.
- She is filled with gratitude and a knowingness that everything happens for a reason, and for her spiritual growth.

As I write about empowerment, I came across a video on Facebook of a young girl I met when I was in India. She had been rescued from a red light district in Kolkata and was trained as a jeweler with Made by Survivors. Now she is working and earning a fair wage.

Feb 26, 2014 Video on Made By Survivors Facebook Page:

In honor of international women's day this Saturday, One of our jewelers tells us why she feels empowered!

"I am empowered because I now have good job and salary, and most importantly that I have confidence now about my life."

Wow, so much insight and authenticity. I thought there would be more differences between us.

In both cases we feel empowerment when we have freedom, when we are living on purpose and are able to contribute to society in a very honest and fulfilling way. We are empowered when we feel confident to be who we are in our homes, in our work and in the many areas of our life. Perhaps empowerment is the same for a fifty-year-old Canadian woman and a seventeen-year-old Indian woman. We both just want to live a fulfilling life.

Take this moment now to write down your own definition on empowerment. When do you feel empowered, authentic and living on purpose?

As well, reflect on the powerful women who have crossed your path. Who are the Yogini's that have shown up in your life and influenced where you are now? The women who have been teachers, mentors and inspiration?

I have had many, many women inspire and exemplify empowered women to me. Though sometimes it is only a brief exchange, other times I witness the strength over years, which leaves me with memories and examples of the greatness of women. I also realize that they may not see it in themselves, instead continue steadfastly on their path being a remarkable asset to our world.

First and foremost are the remarkable and supportive women of my family. My Mother, Grandmothers and Great-grandmothers, Sister,

Daughter, Niece and Friends are all greatly empowered, strong women living purposeful lives. Then there are all the great teachers and mentors whom I love and attend numerous workshops and retreats with. Also, there are the few, quick and divine exchanges that have left me speechless with admiration and great examples of empowerment.

I was on spiritual pilgrimage in India and came out of a temple onto a very busy street that seemed more like an alleyway. A little girl about nine years old, who was walking all alone, stopped and stared at me. Then she asked, (our guide was able to translate) "Did you pray?" I looked at her and smiled. "Yes, I did." She smiled and nodded but before she headed away I gave her a small gift of stickers and a bouncy ball. She took it happily and wandered off down the street. What a light she had in her eyes, she held such strength of character and assurance about her. What courage she had to stand there and ask me if I had prayed. That little girl was capable and independent embodying bravery and a remarkable curiosity. What a connection.

When I meditated on the Yogini's who have shown up in my life there were a few that stood out directly. I see a woman who embodies Yogini as someone who inspires me with a pure and dedicated heart, a spitfire personality and fearlessness. Another who comes to me is the image at the Temple of the 64 Yogini's, of a seemingly broken soul who is lost and unsure, yet there she was in bloody India. Wow, what a warrior to be so distraught and yet contain so much strength and self-confidence to pull herself up and drag herself to India for healing and direction. A third stands in her strong, determined and loving way in constant learning and teaching. She holds steady to her truth and her empowerment leads others.

24

PARSVAKONASANA - Side Angle

Innovative, Extension

*P*arsvakonasana posture finds you standing solid on the ground extending to your edge. Side Angle gives an incredible stretch to our often-neglected side body. Now is the time for you to push your boundaries, go as far as you can and then just a little bit farther, reach for your edge. How do you hold yourself back? What's the worst thing that can happen? We create our own limitations. This card is telling you to go beyond what is normal, into the innovation of the absurd. The sky's the limit; extend beyond average into the sublime. You've heard the statement "do something every day that scares you?" Give it a try, live with courage, advance and expand.

How to do it: Standing on your mat with your feet apart, bend your right knee and rest your elbow on it, palm facing up. Extend your left arm past your left ear, so you make a straight line with your body from fingertips to heel. Breathe.

*I*n 2010, I attended Sacred Centers Annual Immersion with Dr. Anodea Judith and other top spiritual teachers. I was honored and thrilled to be learning and studying with Anodea Judith. I was taking chakra therapy training, bioenergetics and somatic therapy, which continue to be an essential process used in my practice.

There are many systems for working the interface between mind and body, often loosely collected under the heading of "Somatic Therapy." Bioenergetics is the art of moving energy through the body and dissolving body armor. Originating from Wilhelm Reich and then through Alexander Lowen, bioenergetics works with basic character structures — patterns of behavior and ways of holding the body that are inextricably linked. Bioenergetics works to unblock the energy, reinstating the natural flow, thus softening the tissues and simultaneously expanding the mind. - Written by Anodea Judith

During this class we paired up and one person would speak a statement that triggered them, while the other watched the energetic charge as it moved through their body. The support person would stay with them asking questions to help move the charge. I was partnered up with a brilliant, beautiful, insightful and loving friend who is a Doctor of Psychiatry. I recited my sentence and the process began. It had been going on for a while when Anodea came over and asked my partner "has she released the charge?" My partner replied, "I don't think so, look at her face - she is wearing a Barbie smile." Anodea agreed and they worked with me a bit more until the charge was gone and released. What was happening for me though, was that I was extremely triggered by the comment "Barbie smile!" The original charge was released, but I was fuming about being called a Barbie. Through my training I learned – *"When it's hysterical, it's historical"* and this comment was bringing up a lot of old feelings, memories and frustrations.

When the class came back to the circle allowing us to share what had happened. I didn't want to, but I brought up how much the comment "Barbie smile" had annoyed me and how triggered I was. Anodea Judith then proceeded to work with me using bioenergetics until the anger had dissipated. She held up a pillow for me to punch, she asked me where the trigger was and what the charge was. I was annoyed at being referred to by my physical appearance and that I was plastic. I had been trying to prove myself for decades that I was more than my looks and I was ready to smash that pillow. It was a loving, empowering and healing experience as I pushed the charge out of my body.

When it was done and I was spent, we went back to a group conversation. Someone then asked Anodea, what she thought cancer in the body was caused from. She began with a very clear disclaimer that she would never presume to say exactly what she thought the emotional cause of cancer in the body was all about. She said from her experience in the healing field and doing energy work for decades, that she sees it as pockets of anger. "HA!" I announced. I'd had skin cancer on my face. The entire group turned to look at me. What a huge realization.

I had four experiences within an eight-week period that made me speak up for myself, reach out and expand past my comfort zone. The universe pressed incidences on me as I released the deep feelings about my appearance so that eventually I felt comfortable in front of audiences, speaking out about empowerment for women and stretching myself into new and exciting opportunities. I wanted to stop along the way but it felt like the world wouldn't let me and with it I gained so much insight. It was huge as I worked through feelings around not wanting to be seen, wanting to shut myself down, and dimming my light.

Isn't it amazing how the universe moves so much for us to learn valuable lessons? We get hit with opportunities that push us to our limits, make us step out of our comfort zones so that we reach into a new potential. We become innovative and expand even more.

Are you able to recognize these patterns as they came up in your life? Can you stay out of victim and recognize this is for yourself, for your evolution and for your greater good? Believe me, I wanted to blame; I wanted to run away and think that it was someone else's fault. I could easily have gained sympathy.

Though I wanted to blame, to stamp my feet and to hide under the covers, I KNEW that these were taking me to a place so I can do the work that benefits other people. Don't let obstacles shut you down, instead lean into them, feel the anger, frustration and discomfort and go for it anyway. Step up and be seen. Recognize the benefits of getting out of your way and extend towards your greatest innovation.

25

SURA NAMASKARA - Sun Salutation

Prosperity, Abundance

S ura Namaskara is a sequence of yoga postures flowing together that warms our body. Sun Salutation is a progression providing a full body stretch, increased strength, all while creating heat. This series symbolizes life's ebb and flow along with our ability to enjoy prosperity and abundance. Embrace all the possibilities that life has to offer. You deserve the best, so now expect to receive it. Your situation doesn't matter, it is never too late to take courses, write a book or sky dive. Are you coming from a place of lack? Even when life gets low, expect the very finest is on its way. Can you see how perfectly life comes together? The world has so much to offer. Live each day with spontaneity and never forget the immense abundance. Life is always changing and you are able to flow along with it. Soak up all that life has to offer.

How to do it: Stand in Mountain, inhale and lift arms over your head. Exhale, Forward Bend. Place hands on shins extend and look up. Hands on the floor, bring feet back into Plank. Exhale, lower. Inhale into Cobra. Exhale into Downward Facing Dog. Lengthen your breath and quiet your mind. Step feet to hands, inhale hands on shins and look forward. Exhale Forward Bend. Inhale to standing. Exhale palms to your heart centre.

*S*un Salutation is a sequence of yoga postures that you flow through providing a full body stretch, strength, and fluidity while creating heat. In this sequence you begin standing strong in mountain posture, reaching up to the glorious sun. Next you bow in reverence and gratitude to the sun. Flowing through plank, into upward facing dog you land in downward facing dog for some solitude and reflection before stepping forward to rise back up in appreciation for the sun. Repeating and reveling in luxury.

What is your relationship like with money? Most of us have some form of love/hate association with money and our finances. Let's remember that everything is energy and that includes money. While maintaining an intimate relationship with currency we can direct its flow towards what we are passionate about. Whether you have a lot or a little, when we use our money for what feeds our soul, we will feel abundant and pleased.

Align your spirit with your wealth each day knowing wherever we put our energy it will grow. Create an intention that you will use your funds for what you cherish and what will enrich your life and the world as a whole. Our finances will facilitate in continuing to draw in more of what enhances us. We feel better about our flow of money when it is going to what we care most about and inspires our growth. Do you want to go on a trip? Maybe you want to take your parents on a holiday or your children to Europe. Perhaps you want to buy your own home or a dining room set for family dinners. Of course we need funds for the everyday bills and expenses but when we come from a place of abundance we have the freedom of choice.

Take a moment before spending money to make a conscious decision as to whether this is where you want it spent. How does this purchase enhance your life, does it do that at the expense of someone else? Does the corporation you are buying your product from make this product ethically and does this purchase align with your moral beliefs? Since items are also energy they may hold loving energy or the item may not. Only you and your soul can decide what is best for your investments.

Consumers make a huge impact on our society and we can make a difference as to whether a business will thrive or not. I find it daunting to know which businesses are conducting ethically and admittedly do not spend a great deal of time researching this topic. However, I know that if I can pick up a pair of jeans off of an enormous pile and purchase for eight dollars, I'm guessing that somewhere along the line someone is not getting paid what they deserve. As much as I love a deal, I am not going to support slave labor.

While I was in India I enjoyed bartering for items. I never felt that I was being "ripped off". Oh believe me, I know I paid much more for items than a local, but in all honesty I would have been disappointed in their entrepreneurial skills if they didn't get as much out of me as they could. Let's face it; I possess an abundance that many cannot even imagine. I bought what I wanted and felt comfortable with the exchanges, usually leaving the encounters with us all laughing. When I look at items I bought I know that they are blessed with good karma. I can picture the woman sitting on the sidewalk surrounded by her fabric tablecloths and runners. Few teeth in her smile, I pray that my purchase helped her family.

The best way to recognize all the abundance that you have and to cherish your worth is to tap into gratitude. I recommend writing down your list of abundance each day with your morning coffee or before bed. Begin with the most obvious: children, partners, parents, siblings, and family members you love and who support you in your efforts. Give thanks for your job, friends and home. Be thankful for your body that is working as well as it is. If you are going through illness take stock of the positive parts of your body that are healthy as well as the medical and family support you have. Feel blessed with the ability to stand, walk, bend, talk, hear and see.

Extensive travelling has helped me with recognizing the abundance we have in Canada. Let's start with the basics. Having a house, apartment or some structure to live in. Be thankful for having a bed to sleep in, sheets, blanket and a pillow. Be thankful for having hot and cold running water, a toilet, shower and soap to wash with. It's sad to think that thirty-six percent of the world or 2.5 billion people do not have those basics.

Once we connect to gratitude we are inspired to create a life that is nurturing and fulfilling. Gratitude raises us instantly into feeling better about our lives and about ourselves.

Try this experiment, by saying:

1. "Oh I wish that my life could be better. I have it so hard and it's not as good as hers."

How does this statement make you feel? What does your energy feel like? Have you actually started to think about someone specific and does it make you feel really down? What happens to your posture? Now say:

2. "Oh I am so happy! I love my life! I have such a great life, I am the luckiest girl around!"

How do you feel? How has your energy changed? Do you start to feel a little stronger and sit up a little taller, do you feel proud of what you are doing and creating?

This is such a tiny experiment where we can easily see results. Just think about how gratitude affects your whole being and your entire life. The simple idea of, "I love my life, I am super lucky!" will aid our emotional state so that we are relaxed, resilient and happier. We will have less resentment and feel better. Thankfulness helps with our overall health so that our sleep is improved, we are less stressed so our energy increases, our immune system is enhanced and we are more able to exercise and stay active. With gratitude we have deeper, kinder friendships and healthier marriages and partnerships. We tend to be more social and less judgmental. Our career gets improved and with our increased productivity we can manage better, achieve our goals and make improved business decisions. When we are submersed with gratitude we become less materialistic and self-centered. We have a more up-beat optimistic personality and we feel connected with spirit. All of this will increase our self-esteem allowing us to follow our dreams. Gratitude is not a religious state, it is a human state, which will improve our lives and bring us back to a place of prosperity, abundance and appreciation.

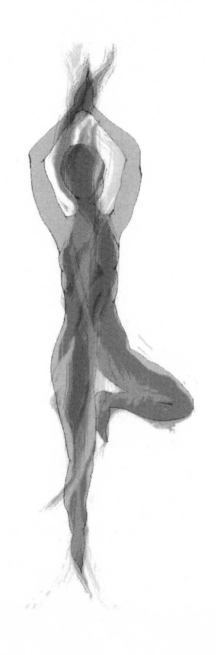

26

VRIKSASANA - Tree

Forethought, Patience

Vriksasana is about standing in a solid foundation where you reach up and out. The Tree posture is about forethought and patience. Like a tree it has periods of growing and expanding with periods of dormancy. Are you able to be patient? During this place of in-action you are given the opportunity to prepare for your next growth phase, a time for planning, planting seeds and forethought. Though it is a temporary state, you have done the hard work and now it's time to be patient. What do you need to do to prepare for your next stage? Would you like to take more training, hire a spiritual coach, connect to a realtor, or spruce up your resume? New opportunities are coming, be patient and have the forethought to be ready.

How to do it: Start by getting your feet grounded, pull up your pelvic floor, tighten your abdominal muscles, and find a spot to focus on. Lift your foot as high as feels comfortable and press the bottom of your foot into the inside of your standing leg (make sure you don't press your heel into your knee). Slowly raise your hands up to sky and bring your palms together. Breathe into your diaphragm.

*W*hen I knew that it was time for me to move away from teaching weekly yoga classes I was confused by this message. I LOVE teaching yoga and I couldn't figure out for the life of me why I was continuously getting the message to stop teaching so many mainstream classes. My husband always said it was crazy how much I love my job. I never missed a class in fifteen years of teaching. I cherish my students and believed that I would be teaching the same schedule well into my nineties. I felt it was the best thing ever, my students were wonderful people who I considered friends, my studio had amazing energy and I treasured the entire process. It was my life, my calling and I was able to live in a fully authentic way that I hadn't before. It was wonderful! So why was I being asked to quit (not yoga, of course) but why was I being asked to quit teaching weekly yoga classes?

I didn't know why and resisted a lot! I had maintained the same schedule consistently for over a decade. Starting by cutting out one or two classes at a time, and adding evening workshops was very satisfying for me. As my weekly classes diminished I increased the number of spiritual counseling sessions I offered. Still the message kept coming - Change.

I kept wondering about this message and didn't really want to do it. Finally, clarity showed up on a weekend Daren and I were moving our oldest son Forrester to Calgary. It was during the eight hour drive that I kept getting emails from people who had planned on teaching classes at my studio while I was in India, were now cancelling. Over the course of the weekend I dealt with over twenty-five emails either asking for or cancelling studio space. I knew it was again a message to change.

The "funny" thing was that I had never signed my lease for that year. I had submitted a year's worth of rent checks and I had verbally agreed to sign the papers, but the Landlord had never gotten the papers to me. First thing on Monday morning, I phoned my landlord and said, "I never signed the lease papers, does that mean our agreement

148

becomes month to month?" She said, "Yes it does." I told her, "Ok I'm giving seven weeks' notice." I explained that I was going to be away for over a month and was struggling to find people to commit to renting the space. Her response surprised me, she offered me a month of free rent. Resistance!

Whenever we make decisions, we will be met with some form of resistance. I believe that this is the universes way of saying, "Really? Are you really **SURE** you want to do this?" When I got off the phone I had to think about it. With a free month of rent it wouldn't matter if the studio was sub-rented or not. What was I going to do when I came back from India? Where would I teach workshops and see clients? What about all my students?

I took the time to think about it, but whenever I thought of keeping the studio my body would tell me NO! My stomach muscles would clench, I got a sensation in my chest and a strong feeling washed over my body that said no, this chapter is done. I knew it was time and I called my landlord and confirmed it. Next, I needed to let all the people know who were renting spaces from me; I thought someone might want to take over the studio. It was a calm, lovely space with beautiful energy. I had almost finished telling everyone and the only person left was someone who only rented the studio once a month. Well wouldn't you know it, she decided to take it on. She took it over two days before I left for India. The entire process was completely divine.

When I returned from India I went into a year of quiet reflection, deep internal work and extreme healing. I took many on-line courses, I wrote extensively and I meditated. I was deep into the power of patience and divine timing. This process has not been the easiest and I found myself reaching out to others for support and connection. I lived fully in the moment and was frustrated with not having a plan for my future. I remained open and had the forethought to make connections while seeds were being planted. I knew I was mentally, emotionally, spiritually and physically preparing for another stage. With forethought and patience I have written this book and am excited to share it.

27

UTTHITI TRIKONOSANA - Triangle

Mystery, Magic

*U*tthita Trikonasana is a posture that requires strength, balance and flexibility. Triangle brings a change of perspective as it opens our heart and pelvis. Embrace the magical mystery of the unknown. We think miracles only happen long ago and far away. Actually, they happen every day to everyone. Have you noticed extraordinary events? Do you experience "coincidences"? What mystery arouses your curiosity? A miracle is an unknowable truth that is unexplained, except by divine revelation. We don't need to know why; we need to ask "why not?" Continue to practice magic. This card is telling you to be open to and expect miracles.

How to do it: Stand with feet apart, turn right foot towards the front of the mat with heel in line with instep of your back foot. Extend arms out to sides and reach over front leg. Keep your front leg straight (make sure not to hyper-extend) place your right hand on top of your right foot or hold onto your big toe. To modify, place your hand on your shin or ankle (ensure not to put pressure on your knee). Rotate your hips as you extend left arm up to the sky and gaze at your left thumb.

*I*t is essential for women to surround themselves and to spend time with other like-minded people. In centuries past women spent large amounts of time together sewing, weaving, gathering and taking care of hearth and home as a community. During this last century it became a taboo issue for women to congregate. Women were labeled as "gossiping old women" when they spent time together and were considered not as productive, even though it would benefit families, children and create loving environments at home. Check in now with some of the comments you heard as a child. What are some of the beliefs that you possess when you think about women spending time together? I enjoy the connection, mystery and find my women friends interesting and inspirational.

Slowly women are making their way back to spending time together and seeing the enormous benefits of sisterhood. Let's consent that it is okay for women to assemble so we can chat, laugh, talk, light candles, support one another, and share ideas. Let's remind ourselves that it is in the greater good of all humanity when we connect and lift each other up.

Add ritual, spirituality and create magic into times that you spend with your friends. My friends light candles, add group oracle card readings, and ask thought provoking questions. Hold your evenings inside or outside adding music, dance and fire ritual. Create a space that is beautiful and magical where everyone gets a chance to speak and be heard.

Some of your group may be super chatty and it becomes a challenge for everyone to be heard. I have seen a couple of options for dealing with this scenario. Make a ritual that each person takes a turn to speak without others commenting or making it a conversation. When it is not conversation then the people listening will hear and not be getting ready to offer their point. Being heard can be a very powerful process and extremely healing. I have been in a group where we used a talking stick. With the talking stick only the person holding the stick can speak. These are both good and effective methods. It offers the person speaking a chance to be heard and allows everyone the power of speaking in a forum that is not conversation.

Take a look at how the men in your life respond to the mystery of you being in a women's circle. Do you feel guilt about spending time with other women; are you being challenged or ridiculed about doing so? Are you questioned and is there suspicion? The unfortunate reality is that often the men in our lives are not completely okay with it. Be aware of the verbal and non-verbal response that you get when you go and spend an evening with other women. Remember that they are coming from those same out-dated beliefs and there is an element of mystery shrouding feminine traditions. A lot of times men are feeling left out, wary, threatened, and uncertain. Take the steps and offer reassurance, so that the tides of change will be smooth for everyone.

Challenges in this area may be enhanced, especially if a woman has just woken up their magical connection to spirit and authentic nature. Perhaps you have been married for a lengthy period of time, together you have been raising your children, both partners are working and life is going along nicely. Then you begin to feel unsettled, you desire a connection. You know you are missing something and you start to open. We often begin by buying books. Perhaps you start to take yoga classes and are meeting new people with interesting ideas. Soon you are becoming even more open and eager to learn. You take a workshop, where you begin healing, learning about yourself and the things that have been going on in your subconscious for decades. It feels amazing and you know you are here to serve, to help others through their own transitions and to be the light in your community with inspiration.

Whenever you do energy work, have a session or go to a workshop it is important to bring your family and the people you live with into your new energy field. After I do any healing work I will hug my children to bring them into the new energy. My dog will automatically come to me and easily get enveloped and when I go to bed at night and lie beside Daren I spin the energy around us both to draw him into my field. I start at our feet and imagine spinning a charge filled with vibrant colors, love and connection around us both. I slowly move the force up our bodies until it comes all the way to our heads and above. On occasion Daren has asked me, "What are you doing? You're making me all hot." I smile and tell him, "Oh, just bringing you into my energy."

Take your light and share with your family and especially your partner. They may not believe what you believe, but as you learn, grow and live a life where you are happy and fulfilled, your glow will radiate. Soon your partner and all the people in your life will be drawn to the new essence. You do not need to convince anyone, you do not need for your partner to be completely on board. All you need to do is to live by example even if you are a mystery to others. Be your authentic self, live from a state of awe and see the magic of your life.

28

MARICHYASANA - Twist

Choice, Elimination

*M*arichyasana and all twists are excellent for our spinal mobility, and maintaining good health. Equally important, twists activate and improve our digestive system encouraging elimination. Now is the time to wring out all the murky parts of your life. What helps you manage? Recognize when you have a glass of wine, a cigarette, an hour at the mall or a pot of coffee to help you get through your day. Do you turn to sugar, chocolate, drugs or alcohol? Have you created a life full of busyness, anxiety and drama? Partaking in pleasure is wonderful when in moderation and not as a coping mechanism. All of these can become addictive; keep us from going inside and doing the internal work needed to become who we are meant to be. We get distracted with outside influences that take our time and our energy. What do you choose? Instead you might meditate, phone a friend, listen to music, or go to a yoga class. Now may be the time for you to challenge yourself, take a risk and strike out on your own. Eliminate what isn't serving your highest good.

How to do it: Sit on your mat and bend your right knee. Extend left arm up to the sky and as you rotate your torso to the right, bend your left elbow and hook onto the outside of your bent knee. Place right hand on the floor behind you. Gently rotate your body and your head. Breathe deeply into your diaphragm.

*T*here are many times in my life when I get overwhelmed and feel out of control. I have a history of creating a very busy, busy lifestyle and it would eventually make me sick. We can get obsessed by these feelings of being crazy busy, anxious and in the middle of drama.

I would plan and schedule in so many activities each day, which I thought would keep me happy and healthy, yet left me feeling overwhelmed. Work, raising children, running a business, exercising hard and scheduling in numerous appointments every moment. Each day was filled with busyness. When hectic, I complained about how much I had to do and felt inundated with plans. I embodied the "Martyr Archetype" and it would feed me. When I did happen to have time to myself, I quickly got on the telephone or cleaned my house, avoiding any second that was not filled with a lot to do. It wasn't a comfortable place to be or to live and I was searching to find some sort of balance. I desperately wanted to feel blessed with joy and freedom but serenity and contentment were scary. I wasn't so sure that I even wanted that in my life.

We can become addicted to many substances such as sugar, caffeine, food, exercise, shopping and obviously smoking, alcohol and drugs. The truth is though, we can also get addicted to being busy, feeling stressed out and drama. It all distracts us from dealing with ourselves. It prevents us from doing the internal work and from looking at what we are here to accomplish in this lifetime.

Yoga and the birth of my youngest son Jenkins, was the beginning of me getting off of the merry-go-round and reclaiming my life. I came back to a very regular meditation practice; I slowed down and eliminated busyness.

At first this was difficult for me. I was used to go, go, go and I didn't enjoy spending that much time with myself. I was not satisfied with what I was accomplishing each day and my self worth was in jeopardy. I reached out to the tools that I possessed at that time including divination with oracle cards, reading books, exercising, yoga, and of course meditation. As well I spent time in women circles to continue feeding my soul.

Eventually I started teaching yoga and I found some semblance of peace. I was happy with my work and family life, living with balance for more than a decade. It was harmonious and it was a wonderful environment to raise our children in. Our whole family was thriving and prospering. Our relationships with friends and family were solid and we were superb parents.

Then one day I thought, "I have had enough!" I knew it was time for me to shake things up a bit. I was now prepared to allow my life to get a little out of balance again. I knew it was time for me to stretch out into the universe and do a little bit more. I felt called to push myself towards an edge that might be damn uncomfortable. I was willing to shake up my comfy and stable life to get a little off kilter with changing my schedule, reaching just a little bit farther and taking the risk to cause some discomfort. I knew things might get messy and I was consciously stepping into that.

I was going to have to eliminate some of the strategies, schedule and relationships that were not serving my highest good. I was prepared to eliminate some of my coping mechanisms that were detrimental and choose to live with more discipline. I took a hard look at where I was distracting myself and which aspects of my life were and were not feeding my soul.

What kind of life do you create for yourself? Can you see how you can shift it into balance or is it time for you to shake it out of balance? You get to make the choice!

Some of us thrive on busyness, stress and adrenaline, while others get thrown into anxiety and drama. Therefore, we all cope differently. I like the rush of having lots of energy and therefore I am drawn to caffeine and chocolate to get me going. Others don't like feeling so jazzed up and instead turn to alcohol or smoking to calm them down. How do you cope? Many of us check out in front of a screen most evenings to numb ourselves in preparation for our next day. Without judgment begin to notice your habits and patterns. Ask if there is something that needs to be eliminated or a different choice to make. Trust your inner guidance.

29

VIRABHADRASANA I - Warrior I

Attitude, Confidence

Virabhadrasana I is a strong yoga posture which engages your legs, arms and core. Warrior I is a confident pose where you are facing directly forward lifting your chin slightly, so as to give a little attitude. This pose reminds you to realize your inner strength and confidence. Do you worry about what people think of you? Are you scared to be too much? Be bold, be brave, and get messy! You know you're amazing, so own it. Right now, look in a mirror and recite; "your name you're amazing and I love you." Do this whenever you look in a mirror, each and every time. Take life head on and shine your light as bright as you can. TADA!

How to do it: Stand with your feet apart, front foot facing the front of your mat. Keep your hips squared to the front of your mat. Bend your front knee, ensuring it stays over the ankle. Extend arms towards the sky. Lift your chin to give a little attitude.

*T*his pose gives you permission to own it! Notice when you want to rebel, scream at an injustice and stomp your feet. Playing small doesn't help anyone. When we don't acknowledge our skills and unique qualities we are sacrificing an element of our personality. I know it's not attractive to blow your own horn, but at times we need to find the courage to own our greatness.

Who do you need to tell you that they are proud of you? When will you be good enough, have enough or conquer as much as needed? Maybe it feels like an impossible force that makes you continue striving for excellence. Look at patterns of pushing yourself and take a moment to notice the people in your life, both real and imaginary, that you are trying to please. Quite possibly they too, are pushing themselves to do and be what they think other people want them to be.

Well, I'm here to tell you that you are doing a good job. In fact we all are. Remember, you get to decide what your dream looks like. It doesn't have to be what society tells you it should be. You don't have to go for the perception of the *all-American* dream. What does your intuition tell you? How do you want your life to feel?

As I am writing this book, I'm sitting in Tom Bird's Write Your Bestseller In a Weekend retreat, typing away. There were many other people in the retreat and we were well into the second day. I was set up on a long table with two or three empty chairs plus space on either side of me. During the full days of writing we spoke very little to the other people in the room and mostly kept ourselves focused to write. The routine was to write for fifteen minutes and then take a quick break (word count) and then we would start another fifteen minutes.

It was midday when a woman who had been sitting somewhere else came and sat down beside me. I had never spoken to her and I couldn't describe her now if I tried. We were instructed to start another fifteen minutes and we both started typing. She was a fast typist and I could hear her clicking away on her computer. Immediately I found myself typing faster and faster yet making a lot of mistakes. My first response was annoyance (fight), I wondered why she all of a sudden came and sat there, next I wanted to leave (flight). Here, is what I typed:

I think that I need to go and take a break. I am feeling this in my neck and my shoulders and I think that it might be beneficial if I go and talk to someone. Or am I over it? Can I keep writing and let go of the ego? I am getting so hot and I don't know what I am writing I know that what is coming out has a lot of mistakes...Grrr what the hell?...Oh boy, the woman beside me has really triggered in me, now I'm looking at competition, the competitiveness in me that just showed its ugly head. Didn't I deal with this, 5 years ago?

I hear this often when counseling clients; they will incredulously stop me and say, "Yes, yes I know, I have dealt with that." As much as we "Deal" with our shadow personality traits and try to change aspects of ourselves that we don't want, they will still show up on occasion.

The fifteen minutes is over and the timer goes, she packs up and moves on. I am left annoyed and aggravated. A spiritual contract has just happened loud and clear, I allowed her to shake my confidence. I know that she sat beside me for those few short minutes so that I could get real.

It was a reminder that all of us have triggers, we have shadows that will show up anytime they want and you won't always be prepared. How do you react? Where does it show up in your body? Because I was writing at the time we got a very clear example of my reaction. I wanted to be better and immediately went into feeling that I was not good enough. I thought about leaving and removing myself from the situation and I felt it very distinctly as heat and pain in my shoulders and neck. This was a perfectly orchestrated divine intervention so that I could write clearly all the steps of triggers and shadow.

Putting high expectations on myself and having a deep desire to prove myself is not a new behavior for me. Yes, I know that about me and it is a quality that is recognized by the people who love me. Daren often teases me that when I go to a meeting I will come home the president. Who I'm trying to prove myself to I will never know. I mean parents – yes, spouse – yes, children – of course, the world – for sure!!! I have been spiritually instructed to add this part of my story since it came very loud and clear as I was writing away.

The beauty of yoga and my infinite exposure to yoga methods has shown me my shadow, how to recognize that part of myself and instead of denying and being appalled by it, I can lean into it with attitude. Don't get me wrong; my first instinct was to definitely not write about this experience. I mean…I would prefer that you not know this part of me, yet maybe you experience this too. Do you get a competitive edge? Does your ego want you to prove yourself? Shine a light on our shadow to illuminate it and bring it into the sunlight. Examine the dark parts of yourself and confidently love them. I can honor that part of myself and I can joke about it at times, and then other times it knocks me off my chair.

Instead, let's remind ourselves that what we are doing is good enough. In fact, we are all good enough, exactly the way we are. This is a complete spiritual truth! We are enough! We are perfect beings that have been conditioned to believe that there are some things wrong with us. The only way that we can counter these thoughts of not enough is to catch them as soon as they pop into our heads. We need to stop criticizing and release judgment of ourselves along with all the people in our surroundings. Use affirmations as a constant form to change the thought patterns that are corrupting you from your greatness.

Let's now embrace and accept that part of us that is strong and motivated. Who can thrive in crisis and is fierce about creating a life full of passion and hard work. We can honor the part of ourselves that keeps moving with authority and drive. We can look at these qualities as remarkable as long as we are aware and only push ourselves to our edge.

I have always known that I would get positive reinforcement for working hard and for striving big, but it was when I went to the Off the Mat and Into the World's™ Intensive and then into the Advanced Leadership training that I began to really and truly identify that part of myself.

My life altering moment came when I had just finished a full five-day intensive training and had moved into a second intensive training. Seane Corn - International Yoga Instructor and Spiritual Activist had us in a yoga posture when she asked, "For those of you who are going from one training to another, how are you showing up in this yoga practice?" More than three quarters of the participants were not doing these trainings back to back but were instead coming in fresh and open. The ones who had just finished the intensive were physically, emotionally and mentally drained.

Here I was in a deep yoga posture and she asked, "For those of us in day eight, how are you showing up? Are you able to take this practice a little easy to nurture and look after yourself? (Nope, not me) Are you able to ease up in the postures and to honor where you are at right now? (No way). Or are you pushing yourself, going a little bit deeper into each posture, especially when I walk by?" (Oh ya, that was me!) Next she asked, "Who are you trying to prove yourself to?" What? Oh boy! Who am I trying to prove myself to? I was trying to prove myself to her, my mother, deceased grandmother and aunt. She asked us if that was truth? Did we need to prove ourselves to that person? No, I knew my Mom was proud of me and I didn't need to do anything to prove myself to her other than to be me and happy. Seane reminded us of what we had just been through in the last week. We had pushed our bodies physically, we had done deep, deep internal work and it was up to us to look after ourselves. I realized I have always, always been working towards getting approval from my mom, other women in my life and then wanted approval from my husband. With that realization I had enough confidence to collapse into child's pose.

Later that day when I saw Seane Corn I laughed and said, "I really felt that you were speaking directly to me." (I actually thought that she had seen me physically go deeper into my yoga pose when she came by.) Without cracking a smile she said, "I would never say or do anything to make you feel shame." Wow, not only did I recognize how I have spent my life trying to prove myself to an imaginary source, I was feeling shame for doing so.

I know in my soul, that both my mom and my husband are proud of me and truthfully; it is about me feeling proud of me. They are also high achievers and I hope they know how proud I am of them. I hope that they and anyone else who can identify with this characteristic knows that the people in their life are proud of them. Please be confident about what feels right for you.

One of the tools I use to keep feeling proud of myself is, I tell as many people as I can that I am proud of them. When a client, friend, or family member does something and I get that glimmer of pride I do not it hold back. I am announce, "I am proud of you!" I know that by saying this they will begin to feel they are good enough. I say it, because I know that they will hold up the mirror to be reflected back to me. The right attitude will make you feel confident. When we have the confidence to embrace an attitude where we no longer need to prove our self to others, we embody the proud warrior.

30

VIRABHADRASANA II - Warrior II

Future, Visualization

Virabhadrasana II is a powerful, centering posture. In Warrior 11 focus your gaze on the middle finger of your front hand looking towards your future. This card represents your vision and how to get there. How do you want your life to look? What do you imagine for yourself? Take time each day to visualize and picture the life that you would like. In some cases we don't completely know what we want, but we'll know how it will feel when we manifest our dream. Create a vision board by putting pictures, words and photos onto a large sheet of paper or corkboard. Collage images of the people you love and what you want to attract into your life, your dream home, a fast car, your ideal body, or the perfect job. Do not fit your dream into your present reality. Allow your reality to fit into your dream!

How to do it: Stand with your feet apart, front foot facing the front of your mat. Back foot ninety degrees. Turn your hips to face sideways. Extend your arms until they're parallel with the floor; bend your front knee so that it is directly over your ankle. Turn your head to look at the middle finger nail of your front hand.

*T*ake this opportunity to imagine what you want your future to look like. Do you realize that we all visualize our worlds to be different and that not any two of us want the same things in life? At times you might think you would like someone else's life, but when you take a closer look you realize you would still make changes.

Since we don't all want the same things, let's understand that there is enough! You HAVE enough to create your life the way you want it to be. You are thin enough, tall enough, smart enough, strong enough, old enough, or young enough. You are educated enough, or you have the ability to become educated enough, there is enough money, enough time, enough energy and enough support for you to create your dream, to fulfill your vision.

How would you like your home to be? Picture your household as a loving, harmonious and beautiful environment. Imagine the walls are painted and decorated beautifully. Envision the lighting to be soothing or bright; however you prefer it to be. Imagine that there are healthy plants, cuddly animals and stunning fragrant flowers in vases on your tables. See a spectacular view from your windows.

Imagine your family as completely supportive, interested and independent enough for you to fulfill your vision. Understand that when you go for your dream your family will also benefit. They will gain because they are willing to give you support and your passion will be contagious. Imagine how else your dream will benefit and enhance your family's life. Possibly your vision will allow you more freedom to be with them, perhaps you will provide them with more opportunities to travel, or your dream will give them more financial benefits. Perhaps your ideas will offer your family a venue to heal, or an opportunity to give of themselves.

Imagine what effect your dream will have on your neighborhood and the entire world. Picture a community where everyone wanted good things for each other. Where everyone is supportive of what you are doing, released judgment and felt happy for you. Envision a world where the population is healthy and content, full of compassion and didn't criticize or gossip. Can you imagine this beautiful, luscious, vibrant, juicy world?

To get really serious with your dream and what you imagine for your life create a vision board. A vision board is where you put pictures of what you would like to attract into your life. Choose images from magazines, posters, photographs, online images, and words and then paste together in an attractive way to create a beautiful and original collage. I always recommend anchoring the vision board with a photo of your family. Use either a very large piece of heavy paper and glue the images on it or I prefer to use a corkboard and pins so that I can keep changing and evolving my vision. Get creative with what you would like to bring into your life.

In the past I would compartmentalized the board by creating four quadrants. One section for house and home, a second segment for work, career and finances, the third slice for travel and adventure and the fourth piece for health and wellness. This approach no longer works for me since my lifestyle; family, work, health and entertainment are all so intertwined. Decide what approach works best for you and then go for it.

Allot a portion of time to creating your vision board. Put on some nice music, light some candles, brew a cup of tea to make the experience exceptional. Prior to this event you may want to gather some magazines that will spur on your imagination and creativity. If you want a new home you might have acquired an architectural digest. If you would like to travel more you may pick up some travel brochures, if a new car is what you desire, go and get some car leaflets. Gather all images that appeal to you in some way and cut them into shapes. As you apply each image to your board close your eyes and visualize what it would feel like to have this in your future. When attaching words, say the words out loud three times; by working with these images and seeing them every day, you make your imagination "denser" and pull your current reality towards your vision.

My next word of warning is to be sure of what you want to attract. It's like the old saying goes "be careful what you wish for, because you might just get it." I have attracted visions so exact of what I have put on my board that I believe it is extremely important.

My most poignant attraction came when I had put on my vision board that I wanted to be global. I pinned on a large printout of the word GLOBAL, because I wanted to start teaching in other countries and holding weeklong immersions. I added an image ripped out of a magazine about India, because I also wanted to go there. Plus I added a photo of myself with the founders of Off the Mat, Into the World™ from one of the trainings that I had done with them. I was a senior leader with their organization and I wanted to continue to work and support their efforts and philosophies.

Within two months of doing my vision board I joined Off the Mat, Into the World's™ – GLOBAL Seva Challenge - India. Something I previously had not had any inkling to participate in. Then within nine months I had raised the money required so that I was going to India. I was thrilled that I had manifested all of this, so I decided to stay past the tour and participate in a spiritual pilgrimage.

It was only a couple of days before I was to leave for India when I walked up to my vision board and scrutinized what I had on it. Incredulously, I pulled out the magazine page that I had put on there and was shocked to realize it was advertising the exact pilgrimage that I was participating in. When I went to sites and participated in the life changing events of the pilgrimage I was in awe of how my future came to be.

A month or so before I was to leave, I was working with the trip organizer to get my flights booked and I told her that I was staying for the pilgrimage. It had been offered to the participants of the Global Seva Challenge, but I was the only one scheduled to go and did I still want to. I responded with, "Yes, absolutely." I was a little unnerved that none of the other participants were going but I messaged Kerri who was leading the group to make sure it was still happening; I needed to get my flights booked. It was, and amazingly there were only seven of us that went. This experience ended up being the trip of a lifetime, where I grew and expanded more than I ever thought possible. I was thrilled to meet and later shared meals with Pandit Rajmani Tigunait, the very sage I had been looking at on my vision board for over a year. Needless to say I was star-struck and now I have a picture of myself with him on my present vision board. I have full intentions of going back to India.

Have a vision board and allow yourself to be open to what transpires. Continue adding to the collage and remove the images that you've accomplished. Feel free to step into desire and receive freely and openly. Release all guilt and restrictive limitations. It is through desire that we take action; remain detached from the outcome to allow the universe to bring you what your soul desires.

Once you have established and gotten a clearer vision of what you want for yourself and your life, see if you are able to put some of your dreams together. The example was that I wanted to be global, make a difference, participate in yoga, be a part of the Off the Mat, Into the World™ community and go to India. The Universe clustered them for me so that many dreams were fulfilled together. Another example of this would be: You want a new job, you want to travel and you want more income. You can bundle these by getting a new higher salary job that involves travel.

Dream and visualize a beautiful future for yourself. You deserve to have your best life ever, and remember do not fit your dream into your reality. Allow your reality to fit into your dream.

31

VIRABHADRASANA III - Warrior III

Ego, Detachment

Virabhadrasana III is a controlled posture that takes strong movement to find the balance. As you shift your body weight forward remember to not over reach. Our ego wants us to be the first, the strongest, the best, though if we can utilize the strength of our detachment, we will more easily get where we want to be. What are you grasping for? Are you involved in drama? When we are concerned primarily about the outcome it increases our fear and struggle. Don't judge your ego because it intensifies your stress and pressure. When we can stay detached we will enjoy the journey.

How to do it: Stand on your left foot with your knee slightly bent. Reach arms up. Extend your right leg out behind you; simultaneously shift your weight so your arms, body and extended leg are parallel to the floor. Straighten your standing leg.

*D*etachment has been an interesting concept for me. Aparagraha is one of the five yamas from Pantanjali's eight Limbs of Yoga. (Chapter 40) Yamas are social restraints and guidelines. While exploring these guidelines I first began to seriously think about non-grasping and detachment.

As a social worker I believed empathy was one of my greatest characteristics and did detachment counter that? I had stopped practicing in a government social work position, partly because I found it challenging to not bring home the energy and issues of my clients. If I had been able to detach from their emotions, then perhaps I would have coped better while I was in that profession.

When I got serious about this idea I found it better for me to call it Healthy Detachment. I started to observe other people who had this characteristic and noticed how it worked for them and the people around them. My greatest example was Daren, my husband. I would marvel, though also at times be annoyed, by how I could be angry or sad and he would not pick up on my same mood. At times I wanted him to jump on the bandwagon of the injustice of what was happening to me. He never did. What he would do was much more effective. Most of the time, Daren uses humor to help our children and myself to pass through our moods. Other times he will ask me if I need a hug? Well of course, who doesn't always want a hug? More often than not he will listen and offer up a varied perspective and an extremely realistic point of view. All of these are hugely helpful and healthier, than joining to create an even larger crisis.

Having a healthy detachment does not mean that you are not engaging. It is when we don't take on another person's emotions and add fuel to the fire. Healthy detachment is when we can engage in a way that is healing, diffusing and creates understanding. We listen and hear with empathy, we know it is their lesson and do not want to take the experience away from them. We may offer a different perspective without attachment. They will do with your observation what they will.

When we go through the everyday challenges of our life and maintain a healthy detachment, then we will be going with a flow where we are not super invested in the outcome. We are working towards a goal, but we realize that life and situations may arise where we might have to re-route or look at a different outcome. This creates so much less stress in your life. It creates openness and an ability to stream along without strife and drama. When a problem occurs we are able to go over, under and around or through it easily. More often than not it is our ego pushing us towards a specific outcome, when we stay detached from the result, we can allow it to unfold as it is meant to.

When I was working towards raising $20,000.00 for the Global Seva Challenge, I extended out to various communities within our city offering involvement. With the participation from these groups of people I implemented events to support my goal.

I reached out to the Indian community by calling a local Indian Restaurant, Taj Grill and Bar, Grande Prairie. We planned an Evening at the Taj where we had a beautiful Indian dinner, a silent auction and included Indian culture with music, dancing and wearing traditional clothing. I was strongly in the flow of the event with little attachment to the outcome. As we were planning The Evening at the Taj, I was unconcerned about how much money we brought in since I knew that I still had a lot of time. This event was early in my fundraising efforts and had many months to raise the money.

The planning of the event went very smoothly. With feedback from the Dream Team, each member played to their strengths, yet were encouraged to lean into their edge. I found myself saying yes to all the great ideas and kept reminding us that it was going to be fun! Happy and supported through this event, I felt detached from the outcome. I was just so incredibly thrilled with how well it was all going.

We gathered silent auction items from businesses in our community and we created posters and tickets. They went fast and furious as we sold out days before the event took place. People were phoning to inquire about more tickets, but we were at capacity. This was such a great evening for everyone. The owner of the restaurant loaned us sari's to wear and donated Bindi's to put on each female guests foreheads. Their daughter and niece performed a traditional dance and the Indian buffet was amazing. I gave a speech that brought tears to many people's eyes. We recognize the abundance that we have and the safety of where we live. As the evening progressed everyone was happy to visit with their friends and feel connected to community.

For me I felt bliss, I was confident and free with living on purpose. I was in the flow and it felt amazing and easy. The event was a huge success. I raised more money than I even thought I would and that was directly because I stayed out of grasping. We remained in a flow of what needed to be done, instead of looking at the big picture and becoming overwhelmed. We progressed with the tasks at hand and moved forward one at a time. I didn't have any expectations and just allowed it to create as it needed and trusted that it would unfold, as it was meant to.

The next event was a yoga conference. Here is where I fully experienced the opposite of the Evening at the Taj. With the yoga conference I was much more invested in the outcome of the event. We received amazing support from the yoga community. I had invited yoga instructors from all over the city to teach or assist in two-hour yoga workshops, which were held at my studio. Participants could sign up for one or two workshops or they could participate in the whole day's events.

I don't know exactly what was different in the planning, but I know what was different for me, was my ego. I really, really wanted the event to be fantastic and it felt like a ton of work. I spent a lot of time in the planning and preparation of this event.

My dream team, who had been so supportive up to this point were all busy. It was not a problem with anyone, life was happening. Some of the dream team was out of town, one was becoming a grandma for the first time, another's husband was having surgery, another got a new job and one had just gotten back to work after being away for two months. Even with all of the signs telling me that it was not the best time, I plowed through anyway. I was met with decisions to make, a lot of work to do, obstacles and really missed their support. I quickly realized, very clearly, that this was going to be a great big fat lesson for me and it was. Being very attached to the outcome, it never occurred to me to change. I was emotionally invested in the event and sought for it to be fantastic! Super successful! I wanted to be the star!

Luckily, the event went well, again raised a lot of money and the participants had a great experience. What was happening was completely going on inside of me, going on in my head, my heart, my body and I really did not like the feelings. It was very stressful for me and emotionally draining. The experience had not felt smooth and fun and I did not flow through the experience. Fortunately, this fund-raising was bigger than me, so that once it was all counted after the event I was only $1000.00 short. This alone was exciting and thrilling. It was September 9th only eight months after making the commitment and I was very close.

The Monday morning after the yoga conference, I absolutely hit a wall! I had drained every ounce of stamina that I had and I was done. I felt like I was free falling smack! Spread-eagled facedown-splat! Onto the floor. I couldn't move! I wasn't in a good place; I felt beat down and paralyzed. My body had started to hurt and ache horribly days before the conference. At one point I wasn't sure how I was physically going to be able to participate in each of the workshops.

For a week and a half I was in Savasana. (Chapter 23) For those weeks I only did what I really had to do, the rest of the time I was in recovery. This was an unusual feeling for me and I didn't know what else to do with it other than to just wait it out. I leaned into it and allowed it to wash over me. I didn't want to get out of bed in the morning; I was happy when clients cancelled appointments and I watched movies and read a lot. I couldn't plan anything and avoided spending time with friends and family. I was not good company anyway.

Then, as quickly as it hit, it was over. I woke up on a Thursday morning and I knew I was back to my regular self. That morning I flew out of bed because I had figured out how I was going to raise the last $1,000.00. I was upbeat, extremely energized and I was excited about what I had planned. Well it never came to fruition because magic happened!

With a spring in my step I went to teach my morning yoga class. As I came out of class, a beautiful soul and friend came into my studio and said she would like to make a $400.00 donation to my cause. This was thrilling. I was extremely happy and thanked her very much. After the studio cleared out, I got an email from a local yoga studio, which read:

Candace, we did donation based yoga classes in the park all summer and we have a $500.00 donation for your cause.

WHAT??? I couldn't believe it! I was ecstatic and elated. The magic continues...

I was seeing my last client of the day. She noticed and asked me about my donation box, when she came out of my office she popped in a $100.00 bill. Holy cow, I was crying and dancing around the studio. I was in shock and disbelief. Can you believe that I did it? It was pure divine magic and I was back to my old self, living in faith, trust and detachment. When we drop our ego and remain detached from the outcome it all gets easier.

32

URDHVA DHANURASANA - Wheel

Cycles, Change

*U*rdhva **Dhanurasana** is a full back bend where you will expand and open yourself wide. Wheel is a continuous posture and when achieved is cause for celebration. Are you looking for an outcome? Are you standing on a threshold? Like the wheel we go through stages in our life. Experience liberation as you finish a cycle and anticipation that you will be starting a new one. This card is telling you it's time to glorify, honor and memorialize your accomplishments. What is the legacy you are leaving? There is a bridge between this world and the spirit world that you can connect to. This can be done through ritual, a ceremony as a rite of passage or a party. Write a letter, light a candle and connect with friends. Celebrate! You are amazing!

How to do it: Lie on your back. Bend knees with feet on the floor hip width apart. Press into your palms, which are on either side of your head. Lift hips and rest briefly on the crown of your head. When ready lift all the way up into Wheel. Modification is bridge.

*W*heel is a posture that people either love or hate. The interesting thing is that the reasons people love this posture are the same reasons people hate this pose. In this posture you will be doing a deep back bend. While doing that, you will be supporting yourself as you expand directly out from your heart chakra. In this position you are exposed and left wide open. Therefore it's all about how you feel; either relaxed, expansive and open or uncomfortable, exposed and vulnerable.

What are the lessons that you were able to learn from this last cycle? What has the transition been and how will this new insight help you into the next stage? What are the emotions that have come up for you as you now have finished? When we go through major changes and transformation, it is our choice as to how we accept or deny the teachings of the cycle.

I remember being in India, sitting in this little tiny room, while the founders of the Dance Movement Therapy organization spoke to us about the progress of their girls who had become teachers. The founders were overjoyed to announce that another one of their teachers was getting married! We all looked at them in silence. They went on to say that she will be the fourth teacher to get married and another of the teachers had become a mother! We looked at them uncomprehending. What took us a while to realize was it is very important to be married and have children in their culture. That girls rescued out of the red light districts would be able to join the cycle of marriage and motherhood was remarkable. My question was, "When they are married do they continue to teach the Dance Therapy?" The answer was a thrilling, "Yes, they do."

We know that struggles will come up at every stage of life, disappointment and challenges that we do not anticipate and we wonder how we'll get through them. Someone may pass away, or get ill. We may have to cope with strained living conditions, moving and upheaval. Continue to engage in your tools of taking deep breaths to keep relaxing your central nervous system, gather information, reach out to friends, enlist professional support, look at your options and remain as healthfully detached as possible.

When we can maintain our concentrated focus we will be able to release our grip on what is senseless and dramatic in our life and remain alert within ourselves. You will be able to avoid delusions about your life and see your world as it truly is which will help you avoid suffering and torment. Lean into your struggles and challenges, with a steady gaze to help you go inside and make the best choices.

When the covering to the spirit world has been shifted you'll get answers. Feel certain of the steps you are taking and the path that you're walking. When the bridge between worlds is lifted there is no question that what you are doing is exactly what you should do and will continue to do. You are on the threshold of making a huge transition, so keep remembering that you are supported through the new. There may have been challenges to go through, yet you know in your soul that your spirit is telling you to keep following through. Your present reality has changed and is all unfolding through the cycles.

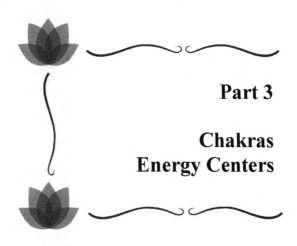

Part 3

Chakras
Energy Centers

33

MULADHARA CHAKRA – Root, 1st Chakra

Foundation, Tribe, Base

*M*uladhara Chakra is represented by the color Red, the element is Earth and the scent is Sandalwood. The Root Chakra is our survival instincts - food, water, shelter, clothing, family and tribe. Do you feel safe and cared for? What belief systems were you born into: Gender, Culture, Religion, Economics, Era, and Geographic's? All these conditionings form our core belief system; as we grow it is our job to question all of these ideals. Notice where fear and an illusion of security might be preventing forward movement. Are your tribal expectations blocking you? Is there a judgment that you are holding on to that no longer serves you? "I have to work hard for money." "If it seems too good to be true, it is." "Someday my Prince will come." You can change these beliefs right now! To: "Money comes easily and frequently." "I deserve miracles." "I am strong and capable." Build a solid foundation at the base of your dream to create opportunity for it to grow and flourish with abundance.

How to balance it: Plant your feet on the earth. Visualize energy moving down through your legs and feet down, down, down into the earth. Imagine tying a golden nugget to the end of your string of energy allowing it to sway with your own rhythm. Now rebound this energy up to the base of your spine. At your perineum picture a gorgeous red ruby spinning calmly to feel grounded, safe and abundant.

"I am safe, grounded and deserve abundance."

189

C hakras are energy vortexes that align the length of our spine. The root chakra is located at our base at the perineum (the perineum is located between the vagina and the anus). Each chakra brings in and expels information. When we connect to our root chakra we are connecting to our families and our tribes effect on our life as we grow from childhood into adulthood. This is the chakra of self-preservation, our foundation and our family roots. What type of family you were raised in, with one or two parents, grandparents, aunts, uncles and cousins all influencing your beliefs and behaviors. Your gender and your family's beliefs around your gender are also a part of the root chakra. Nationality, economics and age all provide information to the root chakra designing who we are.

The element of this chakra is earth, where we are grounded in the physical world. Here is where we do what we have to for our survival for food, shelter, money, clothing and work. We want to achieve and maintain a strong foundation for us to prosper and trust that we are able to support our self and our family. This is when we get organized, keeping our bank accounts balanced and full, our cupboards stocked and our schedule in order. We like to work hard and save money for our retirement, we enjoy a nice home and a good reliable vehicle. The root chakra insists that we get things done and we work hard to accomplish a lot every day. We have high expectations and demands on ourselves.

This is where feelings of "not being good enough" would come from. It is the place where we grip onto the goal of trying to impress others. Here comes the belief that if I keep trying harder and harder, working more and more to be perfect at what I do, then I will get the approval that I am looking for. When or how exactly that belief gets programmed, we will never know.

Chakra excesses and deficiencies are never the result from just one experience. Instead it is years of conversations, comments and actions from the people around us that form the beliefs in our psyche. Here is where we hold our beliefs around material possessions and working with physical laws. As well our ability to have and feel deserving of abundance and identify with integrity and reliability. Setting boundaries, creating co-dependent relationships and our work ethic are all established through our base chakra. Prejudices, discrimination and intolerances are established at our root chakra as the root of an issue.

When I was twenty years old I went on an adventure to travel Europe, Egypt and Israel. I lived on a kibbutz in Israel for six months called Kibbutz Kfar Rubine. It's funny that I can remember the name of it after so many years. I had some incredible encounters during the year of travelling that changed my entire life. This complete experience prompted changes in my spirituality and spurred me to question the beliefs of my family and community.

Living within a Jewish population I soon accepted that I did not have to be Christian to be spiritual and to have a strong connection to the divine. Days before Christmas in Israel, I went to Jerusalem and bought myself a bible with an olive wood book jacket and a small cross that I still hang on my Christmas tree every year. Fortunately, I also learned a whole new ideology. Living on a Kibbutz around people who do not celebrate Christmas was very interesting. As Christian volunteers we were given the day off. Just one Day? In Canada we get several days off for Christmas and as a student I was used to weeks off.

I remember very clearly that one of the Kibbutzniks who were taking us on our monthly tour said. "Oh we respect Christ, (JC he would call him) and all that he did, I mean he was a Jew." I was surprised by his relaxed and flippant attitude about Jesus. What a concept for a 21(I spent my 21st birthday in Israel) year old girl who was raised in a society where as far as I knew, everyone I associated with was Christian.

What I learnt from that experience is that there are many, many people in the world who are not Christian. In fact two thirds of our seven billion population are not Christian. When I was in school from 1967-1980, at the beginning of every school year we had to fill out a form, which asked us what religion we were. I remember we would all look around and not know what to put down. Not many of us went to church and we didn't know what to put on the paper, we knew we were Christian but how specific do they want us to get Protestant, Lutheran, United? Where I grew up the Catholic Church had its own school division. Most of us were another form of Christian, some of us went to church and some of us didn't, but it was all okay.

What I gained by living in Israel is experiencing other cultures and living with people like I had never done before. The Kibbutz way of life is an example of living that enhances community and closeness. It is a beautiful and loving way to live filled with purpose at being part of the greater whole. On the Kibbutz people worked running businesses and manufacturing products, they farm growing wheat, avocados, and dates. When I was there I worked in the dairy farm milking cows everyday and assisting the veterinarian when he was needed. From my point of view it was ideal. Everyone worked in the community at the jobs that best suited their capabilities. Since I was a visiting volunteer, I do not know exactly how they felt nor do I actually know all the details of how it worked. I am just offering this from my perspective at that time. What I saw was a community of independent people who got to experience a beautiful life of community and connection. They had purpose and worked together for the greater good.

My experiences and growth came from living so closely with other people, the beauty of them all working together. I saw cooperation and respect. I also learned about fear, what it was like for them to live in trepidation of a country that was just on the other side of the fence. I saw collaboration and determination to keep their families safe and whole.

When I first arrived at the Kibbutz I found it to be beautiful and peaceful. One morning I went for a stroll along the road amongst the date palms and fichus trees looking out at the Jordan Valley. There was a large fence on the one side of the road with barbed wires around the top. Then there were three or four feet of sand between the fence and the paved road. On the other side of the road were several feet of beautifully groomed sand that butted up to a grassy area. I was walking along in the sand, so I wouldn't be on the road. As I was strolling I heard a vehicle coming, when I stopped and looked it was a jeep filled with Israeli soldiers and they had their guns pointed at me. In the back of the vehicle was a large standing gun and it was swiveled in my direction. They were all yelling and screaming at me. I instantly raised my hands and said "Canadian, Canadian...Canada, Canada" They yelled at me some more and told me to stay off of the sand areas. I was terrified and confused.

I went back to the village area and was told by someone who spoke English that we are not suppose to walk along that road; it is patrolled all day long watching out for people coming from Jordan over the fence. The sand is kept smooth so that they can see the footprint. Oh, Wow! It was a frightening experience and it put the severity of what was going on in their country into a whole new light. I then learned that not too many years earlier, a terrorist had jumped the fence from Jordan, came into the dining room and opened fire, injuring many civilians. As the months went on I became at ease and desensitized seeing men carry guns around the kibbutz, into the dining room as well as all over Israel.

When we question our tribal beliefs and get open to other ways of life; fear and judgment decrease. We become aware and sensitive to other peoples struggles and coping mechanisms. Having a strong foundation allows us to expand from limiting beliefs to grow our compassion for others.

34

SVADHISTHANA CHAKRA – Sacral, 2nd Chakra

Creativity, Sensuality, Intimacy

S vadhisthana Chakra is represented by the color Orange, the element is Water, with the scent Neroli. The Sacral Chakra represents our sexuality, passion, emotions, creativity and desires. Here is where we become intimate and embrace our sensuality. When we are open and vulnerable we go past the ego and detach from the outcome into the true essence of creativity. How do you show your creativity? What brings you pleasure? Are you able to get intimate? When we are passionate all transformation flows effortlessly. Increase sensuality, beauty and creativity in your environment by buying flowers, listening to favorite music, dancing and making love. Enjoy your own femininity by wearing beautiful clothes, curl your hair and apply some gloss. Embrace cycles through the sacral chakra as positive, peaceful, feminine and natural.

How to balance it: Sitting on your mat feel the energy moving down through your sitting bones into the earth, rebound the positive energy up into your body to your second chakra, located two inches below your belly button. See a gorgeous bright orange color spinning in a circle and feel the flood of your sexuality, emotions, creativity and desires. Honor and accept your passion and sensuality.

"I flow easily and effortlessly as
I enjoy and celebrate my sexuality."

195

C hakras are energy vortices located in our body that intake and expel information. They spin in a circle and the second chakra is located two inches below your belly button. Each chakra is behind your organs yet in front of your spine. The Sacral chakra represents our needs, sensations, emotions and desires. Our second chakra connects us to our feelings of excitement, jealousy, pleasure, joy, neediness and guilt. Here we move gracefully and sensually to enjoy the beauty and changes of our body as sexual beings.

Excesses and deficiencies from feeling guilt will show up as addictions, obsessions, rigidity, frigidity, and denial of pleasure, promiscuity or poor boundaries. The second chakra element is water where we flow through our life moving and stimulating our environment with pleasure.

What is your story? What is her story? We know all women have a herstory. It is the story of our progression from child to girl into womanhood. We encounter physical and emotional changes so extreme that the story is written, shared and honored. What is your own personal herstory? Take a moment to journal on these questions:

- What is the herstory you have involving getting your first period? How were you told about menstruation and how did your moon cycle affect you throughout high school?
- What is your herstory around your first sexual experience? Was it a beautiful and truly special exchange? Did he have a clue of what he was doing? Was it rushed and uncomfortable? Who were you able to talk with about it?
- What is herstory around having a child or children? We know that when women gather we often speak and over-share about truly horrifying moments of childbirth. It becomes amusing as we all recite our extreme discomfort and terror of whether a child was born naturally or by cesarean, where did you

experience gas and the joy of a normal bowel movement. You know what I'm talking about. We feel like warriors after giving birth. We share and recite at great length the herstory of childbirth. The torture of breastfeeding and becoming engorged and then the tremendous pleasure that you felt while holding and nursing your baby. The deep, deep emotions of unconditional love when embracing your infant, the intimacy and connection you share with your partner.

- What is your herstory if you chose not to have children or were unable to have children? Do you have a herstory of miscarriages or fertility treatments? Do you feel judged and get bombarded with questions?
- What is your herstory as you age? What are the sentiments that you have with graying hair, crow's feet and a softer belly? Do you love and embrace these changes or do you fight, cry and scream to avoid it?

Take this opportunity to sit quietly with your eyes closed and reflect on those experiences. Embrace your herstory, feel the emotions as they arise. Weep, breathe, and accept your journey.

What is the immediate state of your belly, what's going on within your life, your relationships, creativity, or intimacy today? How has your belly served you and how has your belly let you down? What do you want to embrace and transform? What cultural ideas are no longer serving you? How will you connect with your essence?

What cultural conditioning, outdated views, tensions, ideals are no longer serving your process? What can be transformed?

Pause now and write for 5-10 minutes in your journal.

What did you learn about your belly? Do you feel like you may want to love, honor and respect that part of you more? Did you discover that perhaps you have been mistreating your beautiful and sacred belly? Do you feel like you may want to cherish your belly more and treat her like you would a good friend? Were you able to witness all that she has been through without respect and love? I found this an amazing exercise. I recognized how I felt my own belly had let me down because I had three cesarean sections. I had mistreated my belly beyond what was okay and I needed to respect her for all that she had suffered. I will honor my belly as I would a dear friend.

Here is another hard question to sit with in meditation to hear the answer:

"What is restricting the flow of my creative power, my expression?"

Wait and listen for the answers. Hear what your belly wants to tell you and then journal.

A woman's sexuality has been discussed and revised through every decade. It evolves and changes so much and is scrutinized over by preachers and holy men, governments have made rules for it and people give in to pressures and cultural beliefs around it. The hospitals make decisions on our bodies behalf and we have created such an extreme disconnect that I marvel at how we can come back to our pure natural and beautiful essence of our femininity and sexuality.

What are your own hang-ups, misconstrued or conscious decisions that you have made around sex? Are you presently in a loving and fully sexual relationship? If not do you seek out and feel mixed feelings regarding your sexual encounters? Without society, church, government, and medical influence, how do you feel on a soul level about your sexuality? I believe this is where we need to come back to. In my own experiences I enjoy being in a committed monogamous relationship where we have created a deep intimacy. I believe our strong sexual relationship keeps our marriage healthy, physically powerful and intimate.

When I arrived in this partnership I went into an intimacy like I had never experienced before. I told him things I had never shared with anyone else before or since. My plan at the time was to scare him away; instead what that did for us was to create a relationship that is deep, personal and solid. I feel that because we went there and got so close in the beginning, it has allowed us to keep the intimacy in our relationship. Our connection is cherished and our sex life remains constant, regular and quite frankly spectacular.

If you are in a relationship where the sex is decreasing I encourage you to prevent that from happening. When sexual relations in a marriage decline the soul connection doesn't get recharged. The bond loosens and will slowly start to untangle taking you farther and farther away from each other. Making love is the equivalent of a fantastic non-verbal conversation. You can say and show all those feelings that you have for one another that words do not do justice. It's beautiful and makes you feel fabulous. Cherish your femininity and connect to your core sensuality by making love and being sexy. Explore your creativity to manifest loving intimate relationships.

35

MANIPURA CHAKRA - Solar Plexus, 3rd Chakra

Power, Courage, Visible

*M*anipura Chakra is represented by the color Yellow, the element is FIRE and the scent is Ylang,Ylang. The Solar Plexus Chakra is about having the courage and power to do and be who you want to be. How do you show up in the world? How do you feel about new situations? Do you allow fear to prevent you or spur you on to what you love? This card is reminding you to be courageous in new endeavors as well as to harness your power. It's time for you to be visible to move forward and generate your life. Get excited and encounter new people and new situations. As you step forward take a deep breath to relax your central nervous system. Remind yourself that you are a strong, empowered person so enter with love.

How to balance it: Standing or sitting visualize pulling positive energy up from your feet though your legs resting just above your belly button behind your organs and in front of your spine. Imagine this positive energy is a brilliant, ball of yellow sun. This powerful ball of fire is spinning strongly in a circle, and as it is whirling you can feel and see your courage, power, respect, and confidence.

"I courageously move within my personal power
to ignite my passion and remove obstacles."

C hakras are powerful spinning wheels of energy located along the length of your spine. Each chakra takes in and expels different information. The solar plexus chakra is associated with the element of fire. Here is where we establish our personality and ego. At times you may have a strong, proactive and responsible personality with a lot of confidence and spontaneity. At other times you may find you are gentler and milder with a lovely, playful and warm personality. This is the area where we find our will power and self-discipline to meet challenges.

As this chakra can become excessive or deficient your ego will begin to dictate how to cope with situations. It may take you to a place of dominating, bullying, being stubborn, and trying to control in an overly aggressive way. Alternately, you may find your energy and self-esteem low. You are plagued with blaming yourself and have fear, anxiety and poor self-discipline. You may feel victimized and want to blame others for your situation with violent outbursts.

As I was in the finishing stages of writing this book I took several days to go and stay with a friend at her cabin on a lake. Daren brought out our trailer so I could have my own space to write during the day in relative seclusion. I was surrounded by nature and all of the natural elements. We enjoyed warm summer heat, beautiful blue water and sky, along with a forest backdrop. The days were luxurious and productive.

One evening while sitting around the campfire and chatting, a very large dark cloud turned up. We grabbed our supplies and headed for a sheltered deck. In pure joy we watched the lightening on the lake and laughed at the rumblings of the thunder. We chatted as the rain poured down putting out our fire. It was exhilarating and fun. As the storm passed, so did the time and I headed back to my trailer for bed.

Sound asleep I woke with a startle around three o'clock in the morning. The storm was back and with it came huge power. For an hour I laid almost perfectly still in my bed as I kept counting the length of time between the flash of lightening and the roar of thunder.

I was scared and startled. It was harsh and so quick that it looked like strobe lights flashing through the bedroom windows. At one point the lightening hadn't even stopped before the trailer shaking thunder boomed.

My heart was racing, the pulse in my throat was beating and I was not sure what to do. I had one hand on my solar plexus and the other on my heart chakra. I could feel the strong internal energetic sensations pulsating from my third chakra and at the exact same time I could feel an external energetic commotion from my surroundings. In fact the energy was so thick that I was afraid to move through it.

After I assessed my body's sensations, I went to my mental state. What should I do? What was the worst that could happen? What did I think was probable? Once I decided that I didn't believe my trailer would take flight or have a tree fall on it, I put effort into calming and relaxing my system. I took deep breaths since I realized I was holding my breath between each lightning and thunder strike. I reassured myself and I listened for insight. I stayed on alert as I waited through the thunderstorm as it started to pass.

Once the storm evaporated I was filled with relief and was able to go back to sleep. I woke up the next morning feeling very emotional. I couldn't remember when I had felt that scared before but I know I hadn't in a very long time. My body was vibrating with energy and I knew this was significant. This experience offers a very clear description of how I coped with fear. Tap into your strengths and capabilities and recognize the spiritual aspects of the experience. You have the power within you.

How do you handle scary situations? What happens in your body and what part of your mind takes over? I prefer to avoid frightening circumstances, (I don't like scaring myself and have never watched horror movies) but somehow we can't always do that. The next day I could see how I had gone into a frozen state with the storm, I knew it was time for me to shake it off by going for a run and release it out of my body.

Where does your courage show up? When do you get so passionate that you get powered and fired up about something? It takes courage to release control, delving into the unknown, hoping for the best. Trust your intuition and stay alert for the signs that you are receiving. Use your personal power and become visible for what you believe in.

36

ANAHATA CHAKRA – Heart, 4th Chakra

Love, Joy, Unstuck

*A*nahata **Chakra** is represented by the color Green, the element is Air and the scent is Rose. The Heart Chakra is of course LOVE, unconditional love. What brings you immense joy? Who do you need to forgive to move on with life and get unstuck? What are you doing when you feel at peace and free? What are you most grateful for? Unconditional love is a love for someone, an animal or an activity where you would do anything for them. Thus bringing you joy! When we serve from the heart then the wind blows in our sails. What are you doing when you lose track of time, an activity that fills you up with gratitude and happiness? Who are you with or what are you doing when you like yourself best? Our heart chakra is the bridge between the bottom three chakras and the top three chakras. Love is in ALL chakras and in ALL. Bring love into your relationships, be loving with yourself when feeling your emotions, standing in your power, speaking your truth and following your path. Feel love in all your connections. Only Love Is Real!

How to balance it: Visualize pulling positive energy up through your feet, up your body to come to rest at your heart chakra, located between your breasts. Visualize this positive energy as a brilliant emerald green color. This ball of light is rotating in a circle, spinning in this color you feel and see love, forgiveness, kindness, compassion, peace and gratitude.

"I give and receive compassion with immeasurable love."
"LOVE, LOVE, LOVE"

T here are hundreds of chakra's or energy vortices in our body, yet in yoga we focus on seven main chakras that align the length of our spine. Each chakra takes in and expels information for our wellbeing.

The heart chakra is associated with the element of air and the happy color green. Here is where we experience love, compassion and empathy. Live in a joyous, peaceful and content way with an ability to forgive and devoted to unconditional love. We find what makes us burst with enthusiasm and love of our life. What do we love? How can we forgive? What kinds of relationships have we created in our lives? We can't ignore the heart, because only what is created from the heart is truly sustainable. When you serve from the heart and your dream serves others.

When we look at the seven Chakras we typically see the bottom three as our more earthly chakras. The Root chakra is our physical chakra, Sacral is our emotions, while the third is our ego and power. Then we look at the top three chakras where we may consider them more light and spiritual. The Throat chakra is our will and voice, the third Eye chakra is our intuition and our Crown chakra is our connection to spirit. If we can infuse each of the chakras with whispers of love they will all create balance and we will have a life full of harmony and happiness.

We would prefer to live in the top three chakras, but we need to access the bottom three to get things accomplished and to enjoy the experiences in this earthly body. Therefore, with adding gratitude, acceptance, forgiveness and unconditional love into all of the chakras we can create peace for ourselves that is beautiful, lovely and exquisite. Ultimately what we are all striving for in this lifetime.

We can practice doing this with all of our relationships. Feel gratitude for your friends and family members. Cherish their gifts and offerings. Notice when their personality traits trigger you and see if you are able to look at it from a different perspective and see the blessing in it. Here's an example. I was going away for a vacation with my sister, Vicky. The week before we were to leave, she was texting me information about restaurants and wanted to make reservations for each of the nights we were going to be there. I immediately felt overwhelmed that she was taking control and I prefer to relax and decide at the time where we might eat. I consciously made a decision to release it and let her research where we should go and make the decisions and reservations. Then as the process went on, I soon learned that the dates we were going was a busy time of year and we were having difficulty getting reservations. I completely switched my perspective into gratitude. Thank goodness she had the foresight to make these arrangements, the restaurants that she lovingly chose were excellent, and the ease of it being organized created a relaxing and pleasurable experience. I needed to look at my issue of not wanting to be controlled and even though I initially surrendered, it wasn't until I switched fully into forgiveness as a way to becoming unstuck, that the issue was released. Instead of being controlling and taking over, I love her resourceful kindness.

We can see that we have built in strategies and patterns in our relationships that go on decade after decade. Sometimes we need to take a hard look at the patterns and change our perspective to heal the relationship. Caroline Myss talks about "woundology". "Woundology" is when we use our wounds from years gone to hurt the person who initially hurt us. When we don't forgive and instead use the hurt to keep reminding the other how they still owe us. Come out of the story, acknowledge the hurt, get unstuck from being identified as the victim and forgive.

Our heart chakra really is complex, delicate and powerful. Place your hands on your heart chakra and continuously say to yourself "I love you", "I love you", "I love you", "I love you", "I love you", "I love you".

37

VISHUDDA CHAKRA – Throat, 5th Chakra

Communication, Truth, Authenticity

Vishudda **Chakra** is represented by the color Light Blue, the element is Sound, and the scent is Rosemary. The Throat Chakra is about speaking and following our truth, embracing authenticity, and all forms of communication. What is one thing you know for sure about yourself? What is your truth? How do you express yourself? As a more mature chakra, now is the time to show who you truly are. Allow your authentic expressions to emerge and be heard. You are a unique individual who is here to sprinkle your own flavor into the universe. Sing unapologetically to your own tune, accept your quirkiness and hear the world applaud.

How to balance it: Relax all the muscles in your body and visualize pulling positive energy up through your feet, all the way up your body to your throat. Now see a ball of beautiful ocean blue, this ball of gorgeous color is spinning in a circle out from your throat. In the color you see and feel all your beliefs tumbling around, making perfect sense. Recognize what a unique, authentic person you are. Feel comfortable to speak your truth, honor your decisions and receive with love and respect.

"I live and communicate my truth for my authentic creative voice."

*T*he chakra system is complex and informative systems of spinning pockets of energy that run vertically up our body.

This is the beautiful chakra of authenticity and self-expression. Here we get a chance to sing our song by adding our own harmony. Live your life fully with freely expressing who you are and being who you want to be. I love this idea and it gets me excited to be free and genuine. Allow your light to shine, and radiate a spotlight onto your shadows. Here we can be happy to live creatively with unmistakable communication and an ability to speak clearly as well as listen intently.

There is never a need to lie to others, embellish stories or keep secrets. When you notice yourself exaggerating ask yourself, "Why do I need to exaggerate, why am I not good enough?" With balancing our throat chakra we can overcome shyness, avoid interrupting and stop gossiping. When we do these behaviors we vibrate at a slower speed and feel ungracious about ourselves.

Who are you really? When you take off all of the masks and labels, when you remove yourself from cultural, religious, and family beliefs, ask yourself, "Who am I? Who am I?" What are some of the hats that you wear when at work, with family and friends or out in public?

When we don't live our true authentic self and let our personality shine we are hurting our soul. Our spirit is here to be fully present so that we can speak our truth, follow our path and dance to the song in our heart.

I have worked diligently towards balancing and allowing my throat chakra to live abundant and open. Not an easy task for me, yet something I believe important, so I continue to labor on. What we say, the tone we use and how well we listen are all a part of the throat chakra of communication. Ninety percent of communication is non-verbal, so being aware of not only your words, but also your non-verbal communication, is imperative. How well do you communicate? Are you thinking about your response before the person has finished speaking? Do you interrupt? Are you a chatty person and feel a need to fill any awkward silence? Are you a person who doesn't like to speak, even when you know people want to hear what you have to say? These are all clues that your throat chakra is out of balance.

Be aware of the words we are saying and the beliefs that we are buying into and question if they are fulfilling and benefitting us or hindering our happiness. Ask yourself if this is an authentic expression of who I am, acknowledging that you might actually be hindering your forward motion. This is when you tap into your inner knowing that says, "Hmmm, I'm not really buying that, I believe…"

When your fifth chakra is awakened to the energy center of choice, you will be expressing your truth of your own unlimited joy and elation. When you communicate from your authentic self, you cultivate: compassion, creativity, optimism, gratitude, love, appreciation, and kindness, because those qualities exist in you. Others will mirror back to you and draw in the same vibration into their life. There is no limit to how you can express yourself, live full of authenticity and creativity. I am a voice for the feminine, for woman, girl, goddess, and yogini to accept and love who they are. We are so fortunate to have choice, and freedom to be our authentic selves. Communicate clearly, speak your truth and live fully authentic.

38

AJNA CHAKRA - Third Eye, 6th Chakra

Intuition, Life-Purpose, Perception

*A*jna Chakra is represented by the color Indigo, the element is Sight and the scent is Myrrh. The Third Eye Chakra is about our intuition, following our path and living on purpose. What gift do you offer the world? What keeps recurring in your life, and you are continually drawn to? In one word what is your life purpose? I AM A… You know you are living on purpose when life is easy and synchronistic. Your journey will seamlessly fall into place. Answers are within you already, all you have to do is ask, hear and follow the direction. You will always be given the guidance. Ask your question clearly and specifically and pay attention to your dreams. Trust you will be sent the right person, book or class. Continually follow your intuition to act on those gifts. The more you trust your intuition the more intuitive you become.

How to balance it: Ajna is located between and slightly above your physical eyes. Lying on your mat, relax your entire body. Visualize an amazing indigo color radiating out of your third eye. This ball of gorgeous color is spinning in a circle and you know you have the answer to any question.

"I follow my intuition to my best life."

C hakra means spinning wheel or disk and each chakra spins in opposite directions with the speed increasing from base to crown. The third eye chakra is seeing through our imagination, our dreams and our intuition. With a strong sixth chakra we will have a developed ability to perceive people and situations, think symbolically and visualize.

When we are obsessed and delusional, insensitive, unimaginative and have difficulty concentrating our third eye may be less developed. I believe we all have the ability to be intuitive and to engage with our inner knowing; however, it takes practice and regular use to keep defining it. Increase your intuition by keeping a dream journal, validate all the "coincidences" that come to you. When your telephone buzzes, guess who just messaged you and celebrate that you're correct. Think about someone for a few minutes and notice how quick he or she shows up in your life. Ask to find a quarter within the next hour and rejoice when it manifests. Signs are all around us.

When I talk about divine guidance, for me it shows up as a message that pops into my head. It's a flash that goes across my forehead, but inside my head. Sometimes I hear the words and other times I read the words. It is a thought that comes out of nowhere and is clear and precise. Often the message is only a couple of words, or a quick, definite statement. These thoughts are obvious, exact and kind. They are not aggressive or demanding. On occasion when I am working with a client, I have paraphrased the comment. I sometimes want to elaborate or make the statement a little gentler. Every time that I have done this the client replies, "Oh okay, not sure what you mean." Then when I say exactly the message I received, they respond much differently. They know exactly what I'm talking about. It comes to them instantly as a message they understand and connects to their inner knowing.

I have received messages for myself that I haven't fully embraced or acted on and I notice that I get re-routed. The re-route is less comfortable and can be more painful. I remember, it is always my choice, how I want to do it. I recognize that the messages are from the divine. There is a knowingness that can't be explained or rationalized. Believe me, I'm always trying to explain to others. I sometimes feel I need to justify the decisions I make. I make decisions that wouldn't make sense for others, and honestly, the full picture is often not clear for me either. I have learned to trust that I do not have the whole picture, just my perception of it.

An example of when I got a clear message and only partially acted on it was when our family was on our way home from a vacation in Costa Rica. On the plane the three children sat together a few seats up from Daren and I. During the flight Chloe came to get my camera to look at the photos. I got an intuitive hit that she was going to leave the camera on the plane. As we were debarking, I stopped to look at the front pocket of the seat she was sitting in. There was no strap sticking out so instead of holding people up behind me and not reaching into the pocket to double check, I carried on down the aisle. When we got off the plane, gathered our luggage, went through customs onto a second flight I said to her, "So you got the camera?" The look in hers eyes said it all. Even though we had just left the plane and were still in the airport we were unable to get the camera back. I was annoyed at myself for not following the intuition that had been extremely direct to me.

Guidance comes telling us it's time to break through the surface, make changes in our life and up-root the way things have been. This can be a new and exciting time of changing jobs, moving to a different city or buying a new house. Depending on our perception it is exhilarating or scary as we question if we are up for the challenge. Are you able to see when you are on the brink of your life purpose? As we are entering changes, we'll question our self and the decision we make. It is terrifying to close a door behind us and we would sometimes rather not close the door at all. Even when we know we are being divinely guided to make a modification, we are fearful to close the door. We hold on tight in those cases. The universe takes over, you lose your job, or you get transferred to another city. You get an injury or you find your relationship in a situation that becomes so blatant you can no longer ignore it. Your intuition has been telling you for decades, but the universe pushed you to make the change. We can do it now, or we can do it later, this is the choice that we get to make.

I am troubled that we live in a world where we are not encouraged to read energy. We are told to disregard a clear intuitive awareness. I would love to see us all encouraged to expand our intuitions where we absolutely know without a shadow of a doubt that we are fully supported. Let's all practice and listen to the messages we get from our bodies so we can heal and thrive. When we have to try to explain our inner guidance it's often so difficult and others want to debate it because they don't understand. I have seldom, if ever; gone to a Doctor's appointment where I didn't know what was going on and could tell the Doctor clearly what I needed.

Has this ever happened where you knew certain things and couldn't fully explain it? You slow down your car and notice a police cruiser up ahead on the side of the road. You grabbed your umbrella and then the clouds appeared. We are constantly getting messages and it is up to us to listen and to continue to develop them. Can you imagine a world in which we could say to someone, take a different road home tonight, and he or she would casually say okay. They listen without needing an explanation or making it into a big deal. They don't say, "Why? How come? Did you see something! Oh no I am scared!"

How do you know when you are living on purpose and how do you know when you are not? When I am living on purpose my life is in a flow, it seems easy and I feel confident and sure about what I am doing. I listen to my intuition and I believe in the decisions I make.

Our purpose is not one specific characteristic that we hold, not only one path to get there and is definitely not a destination. Our purpose has many roads and intersections along the way and only when you take a step back or a step out of yourself and take a look at your life will you see a full picture. Your purpose will show up in all sorts of ways and outlets your entire life. Life purpose may come to you easily and effortlessly as something that you enjoy, and you just happen to do. In fact you find that it is something that you can't stop doing. Maybe you've participated in physical exercise in one form or another your entire life so you become a professional athlete. Perhaps it is counseling, or art, dance or telling jokes.

Sometimes your purpose comes from mentors that have a big impression on you. It shows up when you admire a journalist and you become one yourself. Or perhaps you felt saved by a teacher and want to offer this to other kids. Maybe you used to watch an actress or talk show host and decide to head to Hollywood.

Life purpose may come to us through adverse circumstances, wounds and traumas. It is our perception of these challenges that will lead us to our path. A life filled with difficulty and hardship may encourage us to rise from the struggles. As a result we work really hard towards helping others and have a clear calling of what we are driven to do. Therefore, you might get into a career as a doctor, lawyer, nurse, social worker, police officer or teacher. Take a look at your own life. What has shown up for you that led you onto your purpose? How much do you feel you are presently living on purpose and how committed are you to doing so? Perhaps you were an addict so you start an AA or NA chapter in your neighborhood. Maybe you were raped or molested and became an advocate for women's rights. Perhaps you were in a severe car accident and went through extensive physiotherapy treatment so became a physiotherapist or chiropractor. We have all read and heard of people who get clear messages and then made drastic changes in their lives. Your perception and intuition will lead you on the path of your purpose.

39

SAHASRARA CHAKRA - Crown, 7th Chakra

Connection, Spirit, Wisdom

S ahasrara Chakra is represented by the color Violet, the element is Ether and the scent is Frankincense. The Crown Chakra signifies connection and unity with one another, the Divine - our Higher Power. It is about our relationship to each other and knowledge that what I do affects you and what you do affects me. There is no separation. We are all ONE, man and woman. Do you ever feel alone? Do you trust in the spiritual laws? Laws of karma, what you put out, you attract? Think of all experiences as gifts that are encouraging positive growth and connection to our inner wisdom. Can you relate to an understanding that keeps you moving towards higher consciousness? This chakra is reminding you that there are energetic powers at play, trust that you have the wisdom to handle all situations. Trust in your spiritual connection.

How to balance it: Relax your entire body. Visualize opening the crown of your head with a beautiful brilliant violet light beaming down. Feel spirit and connection. You are not alone. Now imagine the light changes to a pure white and the rays reverse direction, floating above your head to rain down loving, united energy over your body, your room and the universe.

"I am one with the Divine"

*T*he chakra system is ancient teachings of spinning energy offering insight and knowledge. These wheels of power are located in front of our spine yet behind our organs coming out the top of the head. The crown chakra is located about two inches back from the forehead. The crown chakra gives us the ability to analyze and assimilate information by allowing our intelligent and aware mind to ask questions and gain wisdom. We can be open-minded and thoughtful as well as deeply connected to spirit. With our spiritual wisdom we can relax into the knowingness and connection that we all share.

With excesses and deficiencies we can at times become spiritually cynical, greedy, apathetic or dissociated from our body. We may have learning difficulties, dementia or confusion. At other times we may want to dominate others while we get materialistic and over intellectualize.

Remember that our crown chakra is our connection and unity. The word yoga translates to yoke or union. When we yoke oxen together they are linked, still individual they support each other and work together. We are all united to each other – humans, plants, animals and the earth as well as joined to universal energies that support our greater good for well-being. We live from a place of belonging, consciousness and connection. Feeling connected to spirit and of being divinely protected.

I came across an angel or a divine intervention was when I was swimming in the ocean in Hawaii. I went body surfing in sixteen-foot waves where I was being tossed around like a rag doll. I knew I was in a lot of trouble and I didn't think that I was going to be able to get myself out of the situation. I felt like I was being pulled farther and farther away from shore and feared that I was being dragged out to sea. I truly saw my life flash before my eyes. Images of all the important and special people in my life popped into my head, I saw them in various scenarios when I was with them. As well as tremendous amounts of fear and panic that I was never going to see them again.

As I was being thrown around by the waves I became extremely disoriented. When I thought I was extending myself up to the surface, boom! My hands would smash against the oceans bottom. It was scary and confusing and in my mind I was trying to figure what to do next.

Miraculously, I got a very clear picture of my mom in my mind. She was yelling at me to get myself to safety, "Get out of there, get your feet on the ground!" I finally was able to get a sense of which side was up, I pushed my feet hard onto the ocean's floor so I surfaced. Out of nowhere, it felt like a strong male grabbed my arm and pulled me. It was the break I needed to catch my breath.

I continued getting pummeled and knocked around by the ocean waves. It was extremely tough to work my way into shallow water so that I could crawl and stumbled my way onto the beach. I wasn't able to walk but as I got away from the waves I was down on my knees, throwing up salt water. It was scary and dangerous. I was young, eighteen years old, and left that experience feeling traumatized. I knew I had been divinely saved. With wisdom, spirit is always around, reminding us that we are important and connected.

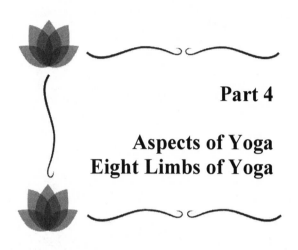

Part 4

Aspects of Yoga
Eight Limbs of Yoga

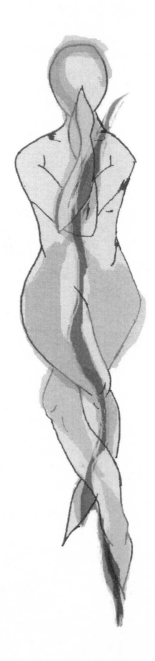

40

YAMAS - Social Guidelines, Restraints

Ahimsa, Satya, Asteya, Brahmacharya, Aparigraha
Non-violence, Truthfulness, Non-Stealing, Moderation, Non-grasping

*Y*amas are described as our social disciplines and guidelines for moral behavior that allow us to co-exist in harmony. There are five specific yamas: Non-violence, Truthfulness, Non-Stealing, Moderation, and Non-grasping. This is the first of Pantanjali's eight-limbs of yoga and offers an opportunity to check in with our moral compass. Is there some area of your life where you have been compromising your integrity? How do you react when someone is politically incorrect? Prejudiced? Sexually promiscuous? Sometimes our ethics get challenged. It is easier when we are around like-minded people. When we are around people or in situations where our personal principles and standards are confronted then we have a choice to make. How does it feel in your body? What thoughts, memories or emotions come up? Discipline takes courage and repetition. Humans have an innate knowledge of what's right and wrong, so bring yourself back to center.

How to do it: Practice, Practice, Practice! Discipline takes courage and repetition.

We all know that the first yama of ahimsa, or non-violence, is a principle of our society. We teach children from birth to be nice, gentle, not to hit or bite. Then as we grow older we don't tolerant violence in our home with our family, friends or with strangers. Yet we can still take a look at this guideline. How hard on yourself are you? Do you push yourself at the gym beyond what is safe and healthy? Perhaps you abuse your body with alcohol, cigarettes, drugs and over-eating. All of these can be forms of violence. Do you only do extreme hot and powerful yoga? Entertain the idea of participating in a yin or restorative yoga practice for a week or so.

How do you behave when you get angry and frustrated? We can show violence to others by yelling and using profanity. Some of us suffer from "kick the dog syndrome". We come home after a grueling day at work, we're angry with our boss, the traffic we've just driven through was horrendous and then we have nothing ready to make for dinner, the kids are fighting and the TV is loud, so instead we kick the dog when it gets in our way, yell at our children or slam cupboard doors. Not only are bursts of anger and frustration hard on our physical, mental and spiritual well being, it is detrimental to creating a warm atmosphere at home and is tough on loved ones.

I went through a period when I was on birth control pills and each month on the day before my moon cycle I would lose it. I yelled at my children and usually had an argument with Daren. I felt horrible and out of control and then I felt terrible about the aftermath. Meditation, exercise and other forms of birth control, stopped the cycle and the behavior.

Violence and bullying in our schools is out of control and desperation of our youth is at a horrific state. Changes need to occur and to do so quickly to keep our children safe and able to grow into confident loving adults. Governments and school systems need to get truthful and real about the problems. For now, we can live by example to show our children a calm way of coping with truth and sincerity.

Truthfulness or satya is the second social guideline. Notice how often we embellish, exaggerate or inflate the truth. Some believe that little white lies are considered okay so as not to hurt other people's feelings. When we lie, it lowers our energy vibration and creates fragments in relationships. When we don't speak the truth there is a specific change in the energy, the person we are talking with will feel it. In truth we may be hurting their feelings more by lying to them then telling the truth since they will suspect the truth anyway. Say what you need to say as gently as possible, tell the truth in a way that won't be hurtful. Be honest with yourself and others.

Non-stealing or asteya, the third guideline, is a principle we are taught at an early age. We know that we are not allowed to take things that do not belong to us. In this day and age we can add an expansion to this guideline as well. We live lives that are full with little time to waste. People who create drama are stealing our time and our energy from us. We all know people who have a lot of crisis and we want to help them. Look at how someone may steal your energy when you try to aid in a predicament. Some people love the attention they get while going through an emergency. Others are addicted to the energy rush of having or fixing other peoples disasters. All are forms of stealing energy, time and happiness.

Moderation or brahmacharya is the fourth guideline that again is easy to feature in our modern day. This guideline directly refers to sex and sexual deviation. The way I look at this topic is that if you feel good about what you are doing and the relationships that you are engaged in, then it is a beautiful place to be. If you wake up in the morning and don't feel good or loved in your activities, it is time to forgive yourself and create moderation. Forgive yourself completely to release any shame or guilt.

The last of the *Yamas* is aparagraha or non-grasping. When I began writing this book I felt pretty confident that I would be able to easily write a book about yoga and the beautiful consciousness that comes from living a yogic lifestyle. Then I got to the writing part and I panicked. I called in my angels, the divine and spirits as I asked, begged and pleaded for them to come and help me. I felt panic begin to rise up my lower back at first and then it moved into my neck and shoulders. I was screaming in my head, "I'm not going to able to do this. I don't have anything new and everything that I am writing about is crap!" This was going on in my head between periods of writing about living in the present moment, surrendering to spirit and allowing me to be. Haha, I started laughing as I realized I was in the midst of a full-blown session of grasping. Grasping for the book to come to me, I was tensing my body and holding the resistance firmly in my neck and lower back therefore preventing spirit to come to me at all. I was caught up in my ego and wanted to do well. Once I gave my head a shake I could laugh that I was doing the exact thing that I was writing about in this book.

Some days we may have to wait a bit, have a temper tantrum, a freak-out in our heads or in a safe environment and then we recognize, "Oh, okay that's what's going on. I am grasping, trying to control, or not being honest with myself." I can recognize this when I am trying way too hard to make things happen. It feels like I am off my center and out of my core. I know when I am grasping because my body gets aches and pain.

I recognize aparagraha or non-grasping when my ego shows up. It is when I really, really, really want something to happen; I am struggling and working really hard plowing through obstacles. Grasping does not happen when I come from my heart or allow myself to go with the flow. When it all seems easy and I am okay with the outcome, I feel more relaxed and not in a panic to make something happen.

This is a lifelong practice for me, so this is my gauge. When I am working towards a project, an achievement or even in a new relationship, I will start towards it. If an obstacle comes up I look at it. How badly do I want a certain outcome? I look at how it feels in my body. I question, do I feel competitive and am I invested for things to go a certain way? Does it feel good or does it create discomfort in my body? Does it seem like a struggle, am I working or trying too hard? Without grasping the situation will unfold in its own time the way it is meant to.

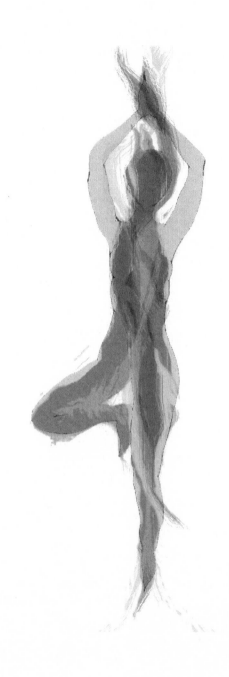

41

NIYAMA - Positive Environment, Observances

Saucha, Santosha, Tapas, Svadhyana, Ishvara Pranidhana
Cleanliness, Contentment, Discipline, Self-Study, Devotion

*N*iyamas are described as our observances and behaviors that help us create a positive environment for our own personal growth. There are five specific niyamas: Cleanliness, Contentment, Discipline, Self-study, and Devotion. This is the second of Pantanjali's eight-limbs of yoga and gives you a blueprint for your own particular development. The niyamas are intimate and personal. They refer to the attitude we adopt towards our self as we create a code for living on purpose. Have you been feeling agitated lately? Do you maintain regular doctor, dentist and optometrist check-ups? Sometimes we put off what we know is good for us; the things that help us create a more sustainable and thriving life. This card reminds us to take care of our environment, it's easier to be content when everything has a place. Look after your health, buy only what you need, continue your self-study and honor your divine. Keep moving and manage your energy.

How to do it: All those things you "Should" do, it's time to do them!

*I*n our world cleanliness or saucha is not something that we avoid, with indoor washrooms and easy access to running water, most of us shower every day and keep our bodies and hair clean and shiny. What is more of an issue now in our present day society, is accumulation. We tend to purchase much more than we need and collect clutter in our homes. I like the rule of thumb that for every item purchased, get rid of an item as well. This is not always observed but when closets and space start to fill be ready to gather items for Good Will. I've become a lot more aware of buying things now and find myself thinking, how I will get rid of this when I'm done with it? We have been contemplating buying patio furniture for an area beside our barbeque for several years. I haven't yet made the purchase because I don't want to get something that I don't love and then feel stuck with.

Notice your own space and clean it up, move things around and take a bag to the Good Will. When we clean out our space it creates room for new. Clutter and excess can slow us down and interfere with our vibration. Keep your home, office and especially your bedroom clean, clutter free and beautiful.

Contentment or santosha is a niyama that I took a hard look at. I like to be moving and challenging myself all the time, I don't like to miss out on anything and I especially like to have fun. So being content and living in the moment has been a challenge. I like to plan for the next holiday, event or get together with friends. It wasn't until I was in India when I found myself living in the moment and content to be there. I was sitting in the far back seats with a friend as she was chatting away about her home in the United States, what was happening with her children and family and what she was going to do when she got home. As I was listening to her I knew that I had to stay in the moment. I needed to stay in India and to keep experiencing what I was, embracing the transformations that were occurring and the expansion that I was feeling. As she was chatting I couldn't join her and talk about my home and city. I lovingly said to her; "Can you come back and be with me here in India?" She stopped in her tracks with realization that she had left. This was a profound insight for both of us. She has since told me that she has caught herself doing that on several occasions and can hear my words to come back to the present. I also hear myself when it happens to me.

This was a new feeling of not making plans and thinking about the future. When I came home from India people wanted to see me and get together. I was strained to make a plan. I would always leave it open and recite that at this time, that day, time and place seems good, but I would let them know on the morning. I was fortunate to have loving and supportive people in my life who were accepting of this. Then I would get together with colleagues and they would be talking about what they were doing and planning. This would make me feel anxious. That was how I used to always be, and now I was sitting here with no new plans, no workshops in the making and no insight as to what I was going to do next. I wanted to feel that way again and thought there was something wrong with me. When I left their energy, I would think, "No, I'm good. I'll keep waiting this out and see what comes."

It was through tapas of discipline and austerity that I was able to remove all distractions. I spent months staying in the present moment, not jumping into activities where my heart wasn't. There were many times when I would begin to start a new project and I hired an assistant to book workshops and classes. After the third session the universe stepped in and the space I was using for my classes was no longer available. I saw this as another sign to listen to my intuition and surrender. Thus I was provided with time and space to write this book.

I created a strict daily routine of getting up early, meditating and practicing asana. Then I set the time for one-hour periods to write. The discipline every day was essential to produce the deck of oracle cards, book and to be true to my next stage of life.

Self-study and devotion or svadhyana and ishvara pranidhana are the piece of yoga that I love and am constantly drawing into my life. I read new books and watch pod casts on spirituality and yoga. I love to keep learning and am thrilled with the abundance of new authors, energy workers, and yoga instructors that are bringing us new and innovative ways of looking at life. Since you are reading this book you are also well into the process of self-study and devotion. Keep it going. Light a candle, burn some incense and feel your connection.

42

BHOJANA – Diet

Nourishment, Hydration

*D*iet is an integral part of yoga. Yoga philosophy recommends eating lightly to attain higher consciousness. Therefore, a vegetarian diet is recommended and ideal. The vegetarian way of eating brings consciousness to every bite. Whole, fresh, clean foods are best. How has your diet been lately? Do you rely on sugar, caffeine, or alcohol to get through your day? Do you take time to cook? Sattvic (pure) foods are the optimal choices for yogis to eat; they bring a calm mind plus a light and healthy body. Observe what works best for you; do certain foods make you tired? Congested? Bloated? Looking after you is what yoga is all about, with diet an important part of creating sustainability and overall optimal health and wellness. Ultimately, you are what you eat! Increase vegetables, fruit, lean protein and whole grains into your diet plus drink lots of water. Since yoga encourages mindful eating, if you aren't a vegetarian embrace Meatless Mondays. You deserve to feel great!

How to do it: Before eating take a deep breath; consciously decide if this is what you want to eat. Do you want salty, sweet, savory or spicy, sour, or bitter? Eat light protein, lots of fruits and vegetables, whole grains and drink plenty of clean pure water.

F irst and foremost the Yogic Diet is vegetarian or vegan. In my yoga classes I encourage students to embrace "Meatless Mondays". I believe all small steps can be beneficial, and by taking one day a week of consciously not eating any meat, brings awareness to your entire family. All mindfulness is beneficial and the reasons you do this can be your own - financial, kindness, health, weight, or environmental. Part of my own personal consciousness encouraged me to become a vegetarian at the age of sixteen, I was a lacto-ovo vegetarian until I was thirty. Due to health issues, I began to eat fish and chicken. Soon, I realized my health problems were in fact due to stress and have since reverted back to vegetarian, though not as strict as I once was, occasionally adding fish into my diet a couple of times a month.

When we eat foods that slow us down, make us feel heavy and unmotivated, we will not have the energy to keep moving towards our goals and our purpose. Notice how you feel after eating meals. The last time my family went for Chinese food, on the drive home I was sleepy and realized eating this food made me tired, lethargic and unwell. Exactly! Food can be energizing or food can be counter-productive to our bodies.

Even if you don't eat meat, you probably can relate to the feeling after eating a big steak dinner or when partaking in the turkey feast. My husband has complained and described the sensations very clearly to me. The steak dinner can make a person feel heavy, weighs them down and can be uncomfortable. The turkey dinner is well known for releasing tryptophan bringing on fatigue. Doing this in moderation can be delicious, enjoyable and tradition. Awareness is key so we can make conscious decisions about how much we want to indulge in.

Sugar can be severely addicting, not unlike caffeine and carbohydrates. We turn to these foods to give us energy and help us to stay functioning. The problem is that they are not sustainable. With the high comes a crash and then we have to add more to get going again. It isn't good for our body's metabolism or our weight plus can increase our stress while decreasing our coping mechanism.

The Yogic Diet

The Yogic Diet keeps your body light and nourished
and your mind clear.

Vegetarian VS Vegan

What is the difference between a vegetarian and a vegan?

Vegetarian: Vegetarians do not eat any meat. Meat is described as anything with a face. Lacto-ovo vegetarians may eat milk (lacto) and/or eggs (ovo). E.g. a vegetarian may eat a piece of birthday cake that has eggs in the cake and butter in the icing.

Vegan: Vegans do not eat any animal products. They do not eat meat, eggs, milk or dairy products and not even honey. This includes food that may have eggs or dairy in them.

Several years ago my husband, Daren and I went on a four-day mountain bike trip. Each morning before setting out we would eat eggs with spinach, mushrooms, and onions, along with whole grain bagels. After several days of riding, my husband said, "I don't think eggs are the best choice for me before bike riding." A light bulb flashed in my head; I would NEVER have eaten eggs before practicing yoga! What was I thinking?

Eggs are slow to digest and tend to come back on people, therefore making your body feel uncomfortable and distract your mind from your activity. I am extremely careful of what I eat before teaching any yoga class or workshop. My normal breakfast consists of a smoothie made with four or five frozen organic strawberries, a small cucumber, celery stalk, handful of spinach, one quarter of an avocado and a scoop of my favourite protein powder. As I move into "wise woman" status I add maca powder to stabilize my hormones.

How food reacts in our body and mind is the reason for The Yogic Diet. What we eat has a huge impact on our body's function, the maintenance of a healthy weight, effect on our mind and our emotions, which in turn dictate how we relate in the world.

If you are thinking about becoming a vegetarian go slow, do not feel deprivation, remember to do what works best for you and your lifestyle, and realize there are a lot of alternatives so you enjoy meals. Re-create recipes that you love and get creative. Try pasta with vegetable-tomato sauce instead of meat sauce. Chop up a multitude of vegetables to get a similar texture. If you normally plan a meal around meat - instead think of the meal as one quarter grain, one quarter beans or legumes, one half vegetables.

So why no meat? Remember that heavy feeling you get after eating a big steak or a large meal? As Yogis, that is what we want to always avoid. The tradition is to fill half your stomach with food, one quarter with water, and leave the last one quarter empty.

There are two main reasons for not eating meat.

1. The first is Pantanjali's Yoga Sutra - Ahimsa - which translates as <u>Non-harming.</u> Cause no Harm means absolutely no harm to self, including during a yoga class, to others, to our environment, and to animals. A lot of yoga students become vegetarian for this reason, for consciousness and to honor their own ethics.
2. The second is to keep our bodies and our minds light, calm, receptive and aware. We don't want to be dull and unreceptive, nor do we want to be over-stimulated and anxious. Our food can affect our emotions and our moods which in turn ultimately impacts our bodies and our health. Our body is how we communicate, interact and impact our world around us. There is no separation between our mind, our bodies and of course our spirit. It is best to keep our bodies light and working as optimally as possible. Your body is your temple...

In The Yoga Diet food is divided up into three categories and it's not carbohydrates, sugars, and proteins. Instead it is the three Gunas - Sattva (Essence), Rajasic (Activity), and Tamasic (Inertia).

Sattvic: This is the purest diet, and the most recommended diet for yogis, or anyone. It is food that calms the mind, yet deeply nourishes the body and maintains it in a peaceful state, therefore enabling the body to function at its maximum potential. A sattvic diet ultimately leads to true health: a peaceful mind in control of a fit body, with a balanced flow of energy between them.

Sattvic food includes: most vegetables, fresh fruits, legumes (beans, lentils, and chick peas), whole grains (brown rice, quinoa), ghee (clarified butter), cereals, wholegrain bread, pure fruit juices, nuts, seeds, sprouted seeds, organic milk, and cheese, honey (uncooked), and herbal teas.

Rajasic: Rajasic foods feed the body but stimulate the mind which can cause restlessness and increase hyperactivity. For people who want a more calm and peaceful mind these foods should be avoided. Rajasic food has benefits to people living an active life where extra energy is needed. Also spices can be beneficial to our health e.g. Ginger helps with digestion.

Rajasic food includes: Coffee, tea, chocolate, hot and spicy foods, bitter, sour, or salty, fish and eggs. Eating quickly, and on the run is also considered Rajasic.

Tamasic: Tamasic foods should be avoided or limited. These are foods that are not beneficial for the mind or the body. They are heavy foods that decrease our energy or Prana and they cloud our powers of reasoning. Some of these foods can lead to mental dullness, depression, or even inertia. These foods have also been regarded as foods that can make us more aggressive and angry.

Tamasic food includes: all meat, alcohol, onions, garlic, fermented foods, such as vinegar, and stale or overripe food. Overeating is Tamasic.

Clearly, living in North America we have a lot of choices offered to us, and choosing the Yogic Diet does not need to be an all or nothing choice. Our lives can be stressful enough so don't cause yourself any more stress or guilt which can be much more detrimental to your health. Instead, yoga is about acceptance. Love and accept yourself everyday and feel the freedom to not get dragged down by your own restrictions.

43

ASANA - Exercise

Movement, Flow

*A*sana is an important part of our daily practice to maintain overall health and wellness. Yoga encompasses much more than only exercise, with asana as merely one of the eight-limbs of yoga. However, when this card appears in your reading take time to re-evaluate your yoga asana practice. Move your body every day to stimulated energy, increase endorphins, dopamine and feel better physically, mentally and spiritually. Do you need to increase, decrease or change up your fitness regime? Do you need to slow your yoga practice down or hold your postures longer? When we move and exercise every day, it dramatically decreases stress and anxiety in our body and our mind. Vinyasa allows our mind to flow with the postures, taking deeper breaths when the practice gets more challenging. As your day gets demanding deepen your breath to remain grounded and calm. Sweat daily. All styles of yoga builds strength, increases bone density, while improving our flexibility. Adjust your yoga practice; add postures that show up in this reading. It is imperative to move your body every day.

How to do it: Vinyasa Yoga is when we link movement to breath flowing from yoga posture to yoga posture. Try Hatha, Hot, Iyenger, Yin, Anusara, Restorative, or Kundalini Yoga. Exercise everyday to remain strong, flexible and well.

*A*sana is the third of Patanjali's Yoga Sutra's Eightfold Path. Exercising each day is not about losing weight or even how great your body looks in a new pair of jeans. Let's not obsess with how we appear and what size we are working at achieving and instead look at exercise as an opportunity to honor our self. Moving your body each day shows yourself that you are worth it. When we don't think we have the time we're putting ourselves lower down on the ladder. Eventually we believe we don't deserve to take time for exercise and then we feel terrible about ourselves.

I don't need to tell you how imperative exercise is. There are thousands of books, articles and scientific studies out there reminding us. What I would like is for us to experiment with this idea, when we exercise we simply feel better. Our self worth increases dramatically since we are taking time for us. We enhance our ability to cope with stress and that will allow us to stay focused and keep moving on with our life purpose.

When we practice yoga we are giving our bodies the ability to stay strong and to function optimally. Remaining healthy improves our immune system and we can put our increased energy into living our full and busy lives. When we spend energy because our exercise programs are not up to par we are not serving our highest good.

Sweating each day gives our body a chance to eliminate toxins. Toxins that we get exposed to everyday from the food we eat, the air we breathe, and the environments that we live in. Add twists to your practice to help with digestion and elimination. Include strengthening postures to maintain strong legs, shoulders and bone density. Do plank and boat to keep your core strong. When you maintain a strong core you will have more agility, which keeps your back feeling healthy and supported.

Start each morning with adding some stretches. You don't have to even get specific clothes on or get out your mat. Stand in mountain posture (Chapter 16) and reach your arms to the sky, add a subtle backbend and then bend your knees as you bend forward to touch your toes. Bring your hands onto your shins and look up, getting a gorgeous stretch through your back. Fold back into forward bend (Chapter 12) before you press your feet into the floor and float back up to standing. Repeat several times.

Happiness in our everyday life really is about our ability to let go of control and allow ourselves to go with the flow. To live from a place where we can move and ebb with all situations that come to us. Our ability to not get mad or bogged down with life and to remain in our center.

I teach a style of yoga called Vinyasa Yoga. In this style of yoga we move with our breath through each of our yoga movements. The type of breath (Pranayama) that we use is called Ujayai. (Chapter 45). It is a strong and heating breath that helps to regulate the amount of oxygen that you bring into your body. It is beneficial to help you stay focused on your inhalations and exhalations as you go through the postures. When holding a posture you can relax and breathe slowly and smoothly into the pose.

The vinyasa yoga philosophy is to allow for conscious movement with an ability to let go and move through our practice smoothly and calmly. It is the ability to inhale moving into one posture and exhale out of the posture, inhale into another posture and exhale out of it again. The idea is that when we do this, we will observe our mind, allowing our thoughts and opinions to also flow in and smoothly out. With practice we can take this ease out into the world with us.

Practice by starting each day with doing ten to seventy five minutes of yoga or any other form of exercise you enjoy. Movement loosens up the body, builds strength and resilience so you will flow through all aspects of your life.

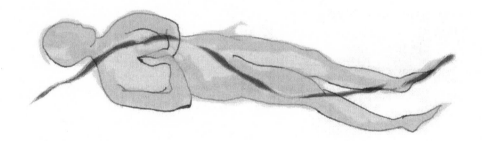

44

DIRGA PRANAYAMA - Three-Part Breath

Relax, De-stress

*D*irga Pranayama is a cooling breath, fantastic for relaxation. Pranayama or breath control can either be heating or cooling to the body. Our society is working more hours than ever, not getting proper sleep and taking fewer holidays. Take a deep breath to slow down and relax your body, mind and spirit. Is there more stress in your life? Are you noticing pesky, little annoyances? How have you been coping with pressure lately? Whenever you experience anxiety take long, slow deep breaths to release the tension and bring you into your body. Do three-part breath every morning and/or evening to relax your central nervous system and release tension with each exhalation. Add deep breaths for a quick fix when stuck in traffic, rushing to an appointment, or dealing with customer service. Practice three-part breath for the next few weeks and notice what an impact it will have on your state of mind as well as your body function.

How to do it: Lie comfortably on your back and place your palms onto your lower belly, just above your pubic bone. Take five long, smooth breaths into that area allowing your lower belly to rise and fall. Next place palms onto ribs and again take five long breaths into your solar plexus area, feel your ribs expanding and contracting with each breath. Lastly take five smooth breaths into your chest. Now bring the three-part breath together by taking a long slow breath to first fill up lower belly, solar plexus, and your chest. Exhale from lower belly, solar plexus and chest.

𝒫 ranayama or breath control is the fourth stage of Patanjali's Eightfold Path. Breathing techniques provide us with an opportunity to gain mastery of the respiratory process. We can recognize the connection between our breath, mind and our emotions. Pranayama can be done with a yoga practice or can stand-alone. You can indulge while sitting in a chair, driving your car, or waiting for someone.

We are exposed to stress in some form or another every single day of our life. Stress is unavoidable, with manageable amounts even necessary. We need to have some excitement and some forms of stress to keep our lives interesting and juiced up. Each day when we exercise we are putting some stress on our body and challenging ourselves can be both exhilarating and taxing.

Managing stress is key to maintaining overall wellbeing and preventing overstressing our selves. By learning techniques and methods to cope with pressure, we will decrease our likelihood of getting sick. There are a lot of methods to help you cope with life. Number one is to meditate daily, exercise is also important and talking with friends is a good release. Seeking counsel and spiritual direction as well as enjoying bodywork such as massage, reiki, and acupuncture are all fantastic to help us manage.

When we can't make major changes in our life to remove the cause of stress, then managing the stress becomes extremely important. Perhaps you even love what you are doing, but it seems overwhelming at times. Create new ways to build sustainability. Dirga pranayama or three-part breath is a breath that will relax your central nervous system, help you cope and bring calmness.

I recommend doing three-part breath twice a day. I suggest practicing it first thing in the morning, then again later in the afternoon, as soon as you get home from work. Doing this exercise is extremely helpful to relax your central nervous system, release tension, stress and anxiety from your body and your mind. This breathing technique can also be useful if you're unable to sleep. Since it is a form of meditation, make sure that you keep bringing your focus and awareness back to the breath. Whenever your mind wanders, and it will, ALWAYS bring your mind, awareness, and focus back onto guiding your breath.

Find steps for 3-Part Breath Meditation on page 308.

45

UJJAYI PRANAYAMA - Victory Breath

Celebrate, Victorious

*U*jjayi Pranayama is a heating breath that will give you energy. Victory Breath is used in many yoga asana practices. The translation says it all Victory! Be proud of yourself and all of your accomplishments. What have you gained mastery over? What are you proud of? Do you deserve a medal? You've stepped up and worked hard, you stayed focused and gained proficiency over distraction. Rejoice and reap the rewards of your hard work, dedication and celebrate. Feel the heat and the passion as you cheer all of your many wondrous deeds. Your dreams have manifested. You have gone big so shine your light! You deserve it all! High five someone, you've got it!

How to do it: This breath creates a sound by partially closing off the back of your throat. Start by whispering, "I'm about to start my pranayama." Now whisper with your mouth closed, keeping your mouth and tongue in the same positions. Continue to breathe long, slow, smooth, steady breaths where you hear the "Darth Vader" sound on both the inhalations and exhalations.

*P*ranayama (life force extension) or breath control is the fourth of Patanjali's Eightfold path. This yoga sutra is reminding us of our connection between our breath and our mind. Since pranayama can either increase or decrease our energy, it can be done with your asana practice (Chapter 43) or on its own to give you energy or calm you down.

Ujjayi pranayama is a powerful breath often used during yoga practice. Ujjayi is translated as "victorious" or "to gain mastery". Victory breath has also been called the "Darth Vador" breath because of the sound it makes. Ujjayi allows you to maintain your power and stamina as you flow through your practice while at the same time creates a meditative quality. As you focus on your breath and continue to move, this powerful breath will diminish distractions so that you can be grounded and self-aware.

In yoga when we get into a posture, we may find ourselves holding our breath. Become aware of doing that, so you can come back to the victory breath. Remaining in this form of breath control helps as we hold poses, we remain connected. When you find the practice becoming more challenging ease up slightly, release a little and use five percent less energy to maintain. Remember the breath is the most important part of any posture. Breath is our gauge to how we are coping and how we may be exerting ourselves too much. Always remember to slow your breath down, take long, slow, steady breaths. I have been told that it takes seven years of regular pranayama asana practice to master this technique. With patience we will get better and better with this procedure.

Take this pranayama into your life as you gain mastery on something you are working on. When you are grounded and remove distractions you can more clearly flow into a project and take it to completion. Notice how great it feels when you cross the finish line, embody the joy you felt when you aced an exam, or created a delicious meal. It is important for us to recognize when we have successfully completed an accomplishment and celebrate each achievement.

Do you ever underplay your endeavors? Do you ever think, "Oh it's not really a big deal?" Yet at the same time you want some recognition. Accept and acknowledge that we deserve to celebrate our successes, to cheer and feel proud of ourselves. Celebrate all of your triumphs whether they are large or small.

When we take a deep breath and flow into one experience and exhale into another, we are going with the flow. Once we begin to get fatigued or experiencing some stress we will slow down. Lengthen and deepen your breath and consciously move into the next experience. Going with the flow regulates our breathing as we continue to focus our mind away from tension.

A friend of mine says that just by giving a high five to someone it changes the energy of the situation. I come from a community where we hug all the time and high fiving was not something that I had ever done. He was speaking at an event and he had all of us in the room stand up and high five each other. It was fun and the energy shifted quickly. It was not uncomfortable like hugging might have been and soon we were all laughing and celebrating.

Since then I have implemented the high five into my lifestyle. Whenever Daren and I go for a run, a bike ride or on a hike, as soon as we finish we high five each other. When I do a project or accomplish a task I high five the person I am with. It has become a fun thing to do, it's easy and it is so true, the energy shifts as you feel like you've done a good job! You have acknowledged an accomplishment.

Let's face it; we often go along plodding through our days and never feeling super impressed by what we are doing. When we actually point out and recognize what we do that is admirable and awesome, it brings us joy. It keeps us motivated and juiced about our next project. We ourselves know when we have reason to celebrate; no one can tell us or take it away from us. It is an innate and inner knowing that yes, this is what I set out to do and I have done a darn fine job of it.

When we celebrate our accomplishments, we feel good about ourselves. When we live feeling successful we will continue to step into our full potential. How do you minimize what you are doing and all the efforts you put into your life? What judgment do you experience when you take a moment and say, "I am doing a good job?" Going for a ten-minute walk, babysitting a friend's child or balancing your checkbook, all of the tasks that we do each day are remarkable. When we accomplish duties, which we may or may not find easy and enjoyable, it is okay to tell ourselves we are doing a good job.

Celebrating and feeling victorious puts us into a really great space where we can share with other people. It is extremely beneficial for our world when we are feeling good about ourselves and what we are doing, so we can encourage others to feel the same. When we are celebrating our efforts we feel happy and joyous. We feel excited to share and to promote others into their greatness. We need to be our own cheerleaders so that we can applaud for others.

CELEBRATE! Celebrate all along the way to keep you motivated and moving toward the outcome of your dream. See the fun and joy in achieving goals and rejoice once you get them completed.

46

PRATYAHARA - Sense Withdrawal

Quiet, Silence

*P*ratyahara is the first stage of meditation and the fifth sutra of Patanjali's Yoga Sutras. Pratyahara is translated as Sense Withdrawal. It is important for us all to take time to be by our self every day with no outside distractions. Are you always on? Are you able to be alone? Can you unplug? This card is telling you that it is time for silence. Being quiet gives us a chance to become aware of what is going on in our mind. Pratyahara is reminding you of the importance of being with yourself, omitting sensory overload and unplugging from worldly demands, so that you can check in with yourself. Remove all external stimuli: television, music, telephone, computer, and lights; close your eyes and spend time in silence.

How to do it: Begin by creating a nice space for yourself by turning off all electronics plus cover yourself to stay warm. Make sure animals and children are settled. Once completely comfortable take a couple of long deep breaths as you consciously relax each of your toes, move your awareness to and relax your feet, ankles, legs then hips. Continue to imagine each individual body part and intentionally relax your back, belly, shoulders, arms and hands. Soften your neck, jaw, face and eyes. Feel completely relaxed from the top of your head to your toes. Ask a question, or set an intention if you like.

"Spirit, guide me so I can be of service to the world."

*I*n our society we are so completely plugged in all the time. We turn the car around to go home if we ever forget to bring our phone. We always have access to each other and we can express every thought to our friends and family. Notice how this may be affecting your psyche. How do you feel when you see certain things or hear about various activities. I know that while I am teaching a yoga class I am away from my electronics for that entire seventy-five minutes, therefore I know that it will be okay for me to be away from them at other times. When I am on vacation I love to go off grid. Consider unplugging. Even for a couple of hours each day, or every other Sunday. Take some time when you don't look at your phone or check your social media.

Find out more on Pratyahara on page 273

47

DHARANA - Concentration

Focus, Unwind

*D*harana is the second stage of meditation and the sixth Sutra of the Eightfold Path. Dharana is about focusing our mind and concentrating on our breath. Have you been feeling flustered, or unbalanced? Are you being pulled in several different directions? Do you have twenty-five things on your to-do list and think the last thing you could do is take a break? When we are feeling overwhelmed and busy that is the exact time to stop and relax for ten minutes and take time just for you. Meditation helps us to concentrate, clear out excess chatter, prioritize and create a peaceful atmosphere. Dharana reminds you to take some time every day to unwind, focus your mind and allow your body to relax as you connect with spirit.

How to do it: Once you have turned off outside stimuli and have gotten yourself alone and comfortable, focus your mind. After setting an intention bring your awareness to the smooth, regular rhythm of your breath. On your inhalation say in your mind "inhale" on your exhalation say in your mind "exhale". Link your breath to a mantra by repeating in your mind "SO" on your inhalation and "HUM" on your exhalation. Repeat. When your mind wanders, and it will, keep bringing your awareness back to repeating either your breath or your mantra "So Hum". Doing this on a daily basis releases stress, gives you more energy, connects you to spirit and helps you to remain fully on purpose.

*O*ur energy can get scattered with our wandering mind and can be detrimental to our mental health. We can get ourselves overwrought with worry and anxiety. We may have difficulty concentrating and an inability to get things done. Focus and mastery of our mind will help our self-esteem. Notice how your mind can get going when you are trying to go to sleep at night, when you're driving in your car or sitting at your desk. We start to think about one thing and soon we're off onto something that stresses us out. With the practice of dharana you focus your mind on one thing such as a mantra, an object, or the sound of your breath to unwind. Use affirmations throughout each day when your mind goes toward a negative thought and focus to call your energy back.

Find out more about Dharana on page 273.

48

DHYANA - Meditation

Between Thought And Sleep

*D*hyana is the third stage of Meditation and the seventh of Patanjali's Yoga Sutras. Meditation comes after Dharana where we have focused our mind. Now you have prolonged the mental focus and moved into meditation. This is the place between thought and sleep. How are you feeling? How is your health? Here is where you can step out of yourself and look at your situation. Where do you need to heal? Meditation is extremely important, and needs to be a part of our daily routine to reduce stress, promote healing and helps us manage in every aspect. Practicing dhyana will relax your central nervous system, decrease inflammation, and increases your energy. Meditation allows us to heal our bodies and mind to develop and maintain complete optimal health, so that we can connect to our spirit and live a full and purposeful life.

How to do it: Once you have set up your environment, continue to focus on your breath or mantra. When your mind wanders, continue to bring your awareness back onto your focus. At some point your mind will wander, but this time you are no longer aware of it. This is Dhyana! Once you come back to awareness, bring your thoughts back on your breath and come into your body. Slowly open your eyes.

267

*T*he importance of a regular meditation practice cannot be said too often. It is life-changing practices like meditation, that will help you connect to spirit, slow down in a hectic world and improve your health in all ways. I have used Mantra Meditation for four decades and the benefits are immeasurable. Guided meditations are an excellent method to help us get started or to maintain the practice.

Isn't it wonderful to recognize how you can have control of your energy? Meditation provides an inner strength and offers you the ability to get yourself grounded, to tap into your sensuality, your power, compassion, choices, intuition and connection to Spirit. You can expand your energy out or you can draw your energy in. You can fill it with loving healing energy or not. With a daily meditation practice acknowledge your ability to heal.

Find out more about Meditation on page 273.

49

SAMADHI – Bliss

Trust, Synchronicity

S amadhi is the final step of Patanjali's Eightfold Path. Here is where we experience a complete connection to spirit, to divine synchronicity and feeling our Bliss. Observe that seemingly unimportant and unrelated events come together that make our lives fulfilling and happy. Are you worried? When we can relax and trust that everything will work out perfectly, we live in pure heavenly bliss. Trust now that there is a merging of sequences that will create your destiny, all leveraging the intelligence of the universe. Trust that there is a rhythm, living in harmony, coming to you with effortless ease. Distinguish and celebrate the cosmic dance. Live in the present moment and recognize all the beauty and abundance surrounding you. When things go right, things keep going right. It seems like coincidence, but when you relax into the flow of life, surrender and trust that you will always be divinely taken care of, everything feels so much easier.

How to do it: Trust, Trust, Trust and then Surrender. Trust that you are safe and taken care of. If ever you're feeling worried, affirm:

"I am divinely taken care of and all my needs are met."

When I was thirteen years old I learned Transcendental Meditation. My parents were busy, hard-working self-employed parents of three teen-age children and were looking for something to help them manage stress. One evening they were watching Johnny Carson (yes, it was a long time ago) on television and saw the Maharishi Maheesh Yogi talking about Transcendental Meditation. They looked into it and arranged for our entire family to go and learn the process. To this day, I am happy and full of gratitude that I learnt meditation at such a young age. We took the course and went through the ritual of being given our own personal Mantra.

I started my daily practice at that time, though periodically suspending, I returned to it again and again. In my thirties, meditation became a non-negotiable part of my life. Having this daily practice helped fill my desire for spirituality and provided me with an opportunity to connect to The Divine. Meditation gave me a way to remain calm in a chaotic world and to hear how I was being guided. That connection allowed me to feel safe and gave me hope. It is an amazing tool that I am so grateful to have learnt at such a young age. It has been more beneficial to me than I can ever express.

The benefits of meditation are huge and important to note. The results may vary from feeling better physically, being calmer and more in control of your emotions, to increased energy and vitality; so expect to see results quickly. You'll have less pain or discomfort in your body, along with better digestion and eating habits. You will sleep better and wake up each morning refreshed. You may find yourself standing taller, feeling stronger or lighter. Your doctor will also see results of lower heart rate, improved immune system, improved metabolic rate, lower cholesterol, lower cortisol and lactate (chemicals associated with stress) and normalized blood pressure.

The results will come quickly for your over-all emotional body as well. You will feel calmer, relaxed and will be more able to cope with life. You will gain focus and increased concentration, along with creativity and mental expansiveness for problem solving efficiency. Your memory will improve and you will eliminate depression, irritability and moodiness. These are all qualities to help you feel rejuvenated, vital and bliss.

When you trust in the synchronicity of life, you will achieve true bliss.

7 STEPS TO MEDITATION

Below are 7 Steps to Meditation: Plan to do ten minutes each day to start and I guarantee you will notice results immediately! Work your way up to thirty minutes each and every day. The only difficult thing about meditating is making time to do it. Don't be hard on yourself, your mind will wander and that's perfectly normal.

<u>PRATYAHARA</u>

1. Get yourself and your environment comfortable, warm and without distractions, set a timer on the stove or phone so you won't think at all about how long you've been at it. Add five minutes onto the timer for relaxation and to settle in. You can add ritual here if you like; light a candle, set up an altar, look at an inspiring image or statue, bring nature into your space.

2. Sit in a chair so your back is supported with your feet on the floor or a stool (make sure you don't lock your knees). It is not recommended to meditate lying down since you're more apt to fall asleep. Cover yourself with a blanket because your body temperature will lower.

3. Take yourself through some relaxation. Begin with a few deep, cleansing breaths before you consciously start relaxing each part of your body. Start to relax your toes, feet, ankles, legs, hips, back, soften your abdomen, shoulders, arms, hands and fingers. Release

your neck, jaw, mouth, cheeks, eyes, brow, and scalp...feel completely relaxed from head to toe.

DHARANA

4. Begin to focus on your breath. At this point you may wish to ask spirit for some inspiration or answers. "Spirit allows me to relax." "Help me with my problem." "Show me what I need to know."

    Connect to your breath by noting and repeating in your mind "inhale" as you inhale, and "exhale" as you exhale. Continue to follow and connect to your breath for ten to twenty breaths.

5. Next add your mantra with your breath. Repeat a mantra in your mind. (OM or SO-HUM or English words such as PEACE or LOVE) I prefer to use Sanskrit words since it doesn't invoke a thought.

    As you inhale repeat in your mind SO and as your exhale say in your mind HUM. Inhale SO, Exhale HUM. Inhale SO, Exhale HUM. Inhale SO, Exhale HUM.

6. Notice when your mind wanders and you start to think about other things, and then bring your mind back onto the mantra. SO-HUM. This will continue to happen throughout the entire process. WHEN (not if) your mind wanders keep bringing it back to the mantra. Our minds are ALL made to wander and be active; this is completely normal, yet with regular practice it will get smoother and easier. Do not give up at this point simply because of this common behavior.

DHYANA

7. When the timer goes, notice how you may have no longer been aware that your mind had moved on, though you were not asleep. Take a few deep breaths as you gently bring your awareness back, you are done. Feel a sense of gratitude that your life has given you the awareness and opportunity to do this for yourself and your family.

SAMADHI

When you have reached samadhi you will be at a place of complete unity and bliss.

You will have gained insight, and knowledge; perhaps you received a message and embody an absolute sense of union with the divine.

Even if you don't experience Samadhi every time you meditate you still get enveloped in the feelings of happiness and contentment. We don't get answers every time we meditate and we don't leave every meditation practice feeling complete bliss, however you will feel good, perhaps clearer and more energized. I believe that if everyone meditated on a daily basis, the world would be a calmer, more peaceful and loving place. Please take time to meditate!

50

SEVA - Service

Community, Charity

S eva is the act of selfless service. I believe we are all here to be of service in some way. Where do you find yourself giving in your life? How do you help others? Recognize and acknowledge how much you do on a regular basis. You give to children's schools and activities, the local hospital, corporate challenges, as well as donations, bottle drives and picking up garbage. You also give to your family, friends, staff, or clients. You give locally, nationally and internationally. Step in to the leadership positions and say, "Yes". When we begin a new charity project it feels inspiring and optimistic, at some point it may lose its appeal, here is where I challenge you to stay with it. How can you create the inspiration to stay with a charity or project when the romance has ebbed? Brainstorm new ideas or change your focus. As much as you give, what are you receiving in return? For every dollar, for every item donated, for every hour, you are rewarded three fold. When you give, you receive through networking, accolades, learning new skills and a sense of belonging. The world needs all that you are doing. This is community. Thank-you!

How to do it: Open up your heart, open up your calendar, and open up your wallet.

I can't even begin to share with you how beneficial and special it is to give to others. The amount I have received as a result of doing the Global Seva Challenge is such a perfect example. I know that I have also received so much from helping out at my children's schools, sponsoring my son's ball hockey team, volunteering my time and being a part of fundraising events. The people you meet are incredible. The passion you witness is amazing and the generosity of your community warms your heart and re-establishes your belief of humanity.

I have read recommendations that when a person is deeply depressed, feeling alone or isolated, they will help their recovery, by reaching out to organizations and volunteering their time. The gratitude from people who receive the assistance is touching. You feel like you are really doing something and your efforts are making a difference. We know that in every center of every city in every country there is need for generosity. The benefits you gain by reaching out and offering assistance will come back to you three, five or ten fold. Be generous, share what you have and offer your expertise. You will not regret it.

When you have an interaction with another person, always strive to leave them feeling better than before. You can offer a genuine compliment; a compliment does not have to be about another person's looks or clothing. Give an accolade about what a good Mom they are, how fun they are to be around and what a great listener they are. Step out of your comfort zone and buy a stranger a coffee or let them go ahead of you in a line up.

Tell a joke to lighten up someone's day. My husband has a fantastic sense of humor and I laugh easily at his jokes. He seems to have no desire to impress people and abandoned the cool factor somewhere along the way, according to his children. He is perfectly fine to be goofy and makes people around him smile and feel loved.

When we go out and about he often says funny things to people we encounter. They smile or laugh and all is great. When we went to Italy Daren was joking with the taxi driver who was dropping us off at our hotel. The driver was very serious and trying to understand Daren's English. Daren kept saying what he thought was humorous and the driver kept trying to grasp it. The funny thing was that Daren took a really long time to abandon the joke and realize that it was not going to go through translation. The more he kept trying to get the guy to understand, the funnier I thought this situation was. Needless to say the driver at no time ever thought he was funny, but we got to share a giggle. Another time when we were on a family vacation in Costa Rica, we pulled into a parking lot. As we were getting out of the car a man walked over and said "Hola" Hello. Daren replies automatically, "Gracias" Thank you. All three kids in the back seat burst out laughing.

Recognize how much you are already giving. Take a look at all the times that you are giving of yourself, quite possibly it doesn't even feel like you are doing much or that it takes much of your time. You may just offer one person some of your precious time and energy; you give an extra couple of dollars for a charity when you are purchasing something. You take a tray of cookies to the office or hospital. All of these things are acts of kindness. They go such a long way in making the lives of others more loving and important. Charitable acts of kindness can cheer another person's day, can take very little effort on our part, yet connects us to our community with purpose.

51

DRISHTI - Focal Point

Vision, Gaze

*D*rishti is the place to rest your gaze with each of your yoga postures. It is a means for developing a concentrated intention while doing yoga. Can you see where you are going? What's your mission? Are you able to look at what you need to see? Now is the time to focus on your vision, release all other distractions, and look with intent. Put on your blinders and remove your rose-colored glasses. Once you have fixed your gaze be aware of resistance that will ask you, "How badly do you want this?" No one said it was going to be easy, but when you overcome obstacles you will feel proud, your confidence will boost and you're sure about what you have accomplished. Don't run away from difficulty, instead take a deep breath and courageously put your energy into it. Take aim...bulls-eye.

How to do it: In every yoga posture there is a place to focus: Middle finger, hand, thumb, third eye, tip of the nose, either side, above towards the sky, the navel or our toes. Doing this in each asana provides you an opportunity to go inside and stay focused in the present moment.

*H*aving a drishti or focal point is really about putting blinders on and going for what you want. You have a gaze that is spearheaded onto a vision and there is nothing that needs to get in your way. Here is where you see all challenges as opportunities. Life can be like a game and you are happy to move the pieces around for you to acquire the outcome your soul demands. You are able to breathe into the discomfort and know that it will be temporary. You move to the next position and re-focus your gaze onto the new spot.

How are you at problem solving? When resistance and obstacles show themselves do you want to stop, not do it and settle for something else? Many times while writing this book I kept thinking, "you know, I could just drop the whole idea and see if I could get a job at Starbucks." Even as I write this I think, if they would hire me, that is still definitely an option. I could work three or four shifts a week, get to chat with people and give them a cup of joy. In spite of this, each day I made time to write and edit my book, plus go grab a coffee from Starbucks. Though I had a clear vision, I maintained one step at a time. I set my gaze to the next phase of what needed to get done and did it. Eventually it must have gotten to a place where you are now reading this book.

Take a moment to focus on your vision. Take a deep breath and allow yourself to stay where you are but use five percent less energy. Relax the muscles in your shoulders, soften your face and remind yourself that you have this. This challenge will increase your self-assurance and teach you how to handle difficult situations. The accomplishment will make you feel proud and confident.

When we take obstacles and deal with them honestly and head on, we can feel really pleased with ourselves. We can hold our head up high, look people directly in the eye and know that we have done the best that we could. We have not taken an easy way out and aborted our plan, we have held our gaze strong and true to our vision. Focus your gaze, center your energy and shoot it towards your vision.

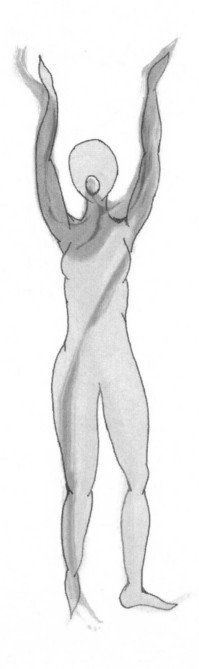

52

CHANTING - Sound

Om, Vibration

*O*m is a sacred universal mantra that all sounds resonate from. Since the dawn of time humans have been using Sound to communicate, heal and transform. Chanting allows for an opportunity to find your voice and to spread it out to the universe. We are all made up of molecules and when we speak or chant, the sound vibrates through our body's particles shaking them up and allowing them to expand and resettle. Chanting various mantras creates calming, healing, and inspiring vibrations. It can help us to center ourselves physically and mentally, as well as connecting spiritually. Chanting clears out vibrations that are resonating ineffectively and the repetition joins us into union - YOGA.

How to do it: Take a deep breath into your diaphragm. As you exhale, draw your diaphragm in, open your mouth wide and allow sound to resonate out.

*A*ll sound carries vibration with it, which touches every cell in our body. We not only perceive sounds with our ears but also within each body part. When we chant out a sound from the base of our diaphragm it will shake up and tremble all of our body's molecules. It will expand them out and then allow them to resettle in a pleasing way.

All sounds and words hold energy within them. Some words have a denser, heavier and less pleasing vibration than other words. Each sound and word will have an effect on our mental state, spiritual connection as well as our body. Sound vibration interacts with our physical and energetic bodies in their own way. Introducing new pleasing sounds can open and expand constricted areas, as well as cleanse and release blockages. Sound enhancement is wonderful for deep relaxation to heal physical, emotional and spiritual effects from stress and imbalances.

Sound therapy is an excellent form of healing to change old patterns of behavior and limited ways of thinking. Vibration clears negative energy allowing us to connect to our higher self. Chanting Om helps in recovering from illness, trauma and life changes.

Crystal bowls, gongs, chimes, all musical instruments, singing, toning and especially chanting are excellent forms of healing and preserving joy and happiness. Whenever I am in a low place and I put on music, my mood lifts. When I am feeling melancholy, putting on emotional music will help me heal and move through my emotions. I have a wonderful friend who has built a dome at her home to offer Sound Therapy. It provides an incredible healing and nurturing space to bathe and regenerate cells in the vibrations.

Certain mantra can be chanted to offer further healing and empowerment. Mantra is derived from the Sanskrit word: Man, meaning mind and Tra, meaning release. Mantra can be recited out loud and can become melody, or repeating mantra in your mind is equally or more effective.

OM chanted at the beginning and end of yoga. Doing this ritual brings us into present moment and in alignment with the universes harmonic resonance. **OM** is chanted AUM as three syllables and each of those syllables can represent:

1. Past, Present, Future.
2. Body, Mind, Spirit.
3. Awake, Dream, Meditative.
4. Maiden, Mother, Crone (Wise Woman).

At the end of chanting the sound OM is a fourth aspect, which is a pause in silence that represents something more...Unity.

Here are a few of my favorite Chants:

- The Compassion Mantra: ***Om Mani Padme Hum*** Praise to the Jewel in the Lotus.
- Honoring your inner self and your true identity Mantra: ***Om Namah Shivaya*** I bow to Shiva.
- Mantra for New Beginnings: ***Om Gum Ganapatayei Namaha*** Om and Salutations to Ganesh who is the Elephant faced God known for wisdom, success and the remover of obstacles.
- Honoring the Great Mother: ***Om Shri Shriyaye Namaha*** We honor the creative power of the great Mother, the creative feminine power within each of us.

Chanting is an extremely positive way to heal and to connect with the divine. Make an offering of a Chant or enjoy sound vibration therapy in the form that is most pleasing to you.

53

MUDRA – Gesture

Energy, Symbolic

M udra is a symbolic hand or body gesture that allows the flow of energy to change or enhance. When we make the gesture of bringing the tip of our pointer finger to the tip of our thumb we are allowing the cycle of energy to continue. How aware are you at reading other peoples energy? Are you able to change the atmosphere of a room? Everything in this world is made up of energy and all day long we are reading and feeling vibes. Have you ever been in a great mood and then someone walks in and your mood turns instantaneously? You are picking up on their energy and gestures. Has this been happening to you a lot lately? When we feel a need to protect ourselves around other people's energies it may show up as weight fluctuation. When you feel strong emotions or frequent emotional changes, ask yourself, "Is this mine?" If it's not, then consciously let it go, shake out your hands to literally "shake it off". Imagine swiping another's unwanted energy off of your shoulders. Call your energy back into your core preventing it from getting scattered.

How to do it: Bring your hands into Jnana Mudra by bringing the tip of your pointer finger and thumb together. This is the mudra of knowledge. Rotate your palms down to get more grounded or turn your palms up to receive wisdom.

*A*s long as I can remember I would get energy running through my body. My body would vibrate. It didn't necessarily visibly shake, but instead it was an internal vibration, which felt like I had no control over it. I would associate it with being nervous, especially when I was a teenager. As I got older this would continue to happen, sometimes preventing me from doing things.

When I became a social worker I noticed it would occur after seeing certain clients. I remember coming out a client's home and sitting in my car, my body was vibrating and I vowed not drink coffee again. At other times I would think that I was getting low blood sugar or that I was under stress. Sometimes I thought it was premenstrual syndrome or I was on my moon cycle.

It took many years for me to realize that I was picking up on energy. Energy of the room, energy of the situation and most definitely energy of people I was around. I continue to get this, but now embrace it. I lean into it and recognize, wow there is a lot of energy moving here. Perhaps I'm moving it and sometimes I'm not.

Energy is very, very real and affects everyone in our society. When we notice and read prana (energy) we can identify what is ours or not ours. Some people can feel it more accurately than others, but the truth is we can all feel it. Sometimes we don't know what it is, or where it is coming from and often we don't know what to do with it.

Have you ever been in your home after a fantastic day? You are happily making supper and a child is chatting with you and working on their homework. You are joyfully anticipating the arrival of another member of your household; child, parent, partner or spouse. As anticipated he or she walks into the house and within mere seconds of the door opening, the energy in the household shifts. It is physically like a light was either switched on or off. The shift is so strong that you and your child look at each other. They are gauging how you are going to react to this shift. How many times have you felt this?

Sometimes you can hear the car drive up and the energy starts to alter at that point. Other times you might have to make physical contact, but bam! Now what? How do you handle this change of energy?

Are you able to recognize these energy shifts? If not, pay close attention to it and see if you can create a situation where you will notice it. Go into the grocery store or next time you're walking in the mall or airport and notice what energies you are picking up. Ask your roommate or partner to come into the room in a "bad mood"; they don't have to do anything like slamming a door or grunting. They can just be pretending, but they are imagining a situation that really angered them. What do you feel, what is your first instinct on how you are going to deal with it?

This will tell you a lot. Are you insulated from their bad mood? Can you detach in a healthy way and allow them to have their space but stay in your own energy and remain happy and joyful? Can your child? Or do you instantly go into nurturing? Do you go into information gathering? Do you join them and get mad too? Recognize what happens, without judgment. Just notice with awareness. Can you stay in your center and not get shaken and rattled? This is very insightful; because we are picking up other peoples energies all day long and everywhere we go. Some people pick up more than others and we all have a unique way of dealing with it. So notice, be aware and gain insight for yourself on how you are reacting. Teach your children and talk to your partners and co-workers on how they are picking up on other peoples energies and it is not theirs.

When we continue to do this without coping in a positive way or without recognizing that it's not our issue, this can have a negative effect on us. We can get shut down, disengage with people all together, we can close ourselves off from living a full and fulfilling life and it can make us sick. It will eventually create dis ease in our bodies and our minds. Ultimately, we have chosen that person, job or situation and since we chose it we can also change it.

We can symbolically clear away unwanted energy by shaking it out from the ends of our fingers, sweeping the energy off of our shoulders or taking a shower and washing it down the drain. With practice we can eventually make smaller gestures to gain the effective results.

This means living with the discipline of being connected to spirit. When the realities of our life distract us, we can bring ourselves back to our center. It's important we keep bringing ourselves back to our core and our greatness because it's the place where we are happiest. When we allow our thoughts and feelings to get scattered, we find ourselves wasting a lot of energy. We lose our power by fragmenting our energy. Envision that when you get up each morning you are given a certain amount or percentage of energy that you need to get yourself joyfully and abundantly through your day.

I am paraphrasing the following information and analogy from Caroline Myss: Let's imagine that every morning we are given $100.00 worth of energy. As you are walking to the bathroom you stub your toe, you hop around feeling annoyed, hurt and frustrated. This experience automatically will use up a percentage of your energy. It is up to you how much. When you think, "Oh yeah, this is the start of a great day!" You are expelling even more of your energy. If you think to yourself instead, "Wow, that really hurt, but it's not broken and it will be okay." You have fragmented less of your energy. So here you have either used up fifteen dollars or two dollars. Now bring your energy back to your center.

Next you are blow-drying your hair (this is the place my mind really seems to stray) and a memory pops into your mind of some guy that sat behind you in eleventh grade who made a crappy comment about your hair. All of a sudden, you are giving that very old memory and the thoughts about your hair, more of your energy; let's say ten dollars. You are driving to work and on route another vehicle cuts you off. It makes you frustrated and you talk out loud about what a terrible driver he is, you might even give him the finger under the dash. You have now given away another ten dollars of your energy and you haven't even gotten to work yet! So what happens? You actually NEED the $100.00 of energy to joyfully and abundantly live through your day and now you have expelled thirty five dollars of that energy. What has to compromise?

First, you will compromise your creativity, the number one thing that goes. You may be thinking, "Oh, that's okay, I'm not really that creative anyway." The reality is we are all creative beings and we use our creativity in all sorts of ways, including decision making and following our purpose. Embracing our creativity will create more joy and happiness in our lives. Creativity is the source of productivity, imagination and resourcefulness. If our creativity stops we become robots going through the mundane and never finding any joy in life.

The next thing that gets compromised is our relationships. In our super busy, hardworking society it is our relationships and spending quality time with friends and family that enriches our soul. When we are sacrificing spending time with family and friends, we are compromising our ability to have a life of abundance, freedom and connection.

Our health is the next thing to go. When we expend energy into areas of our life that do not require it, when we waste our energy, it will soon start to compromise our health. Years of sacrificing our creativity and relationships will catch up to us. We will feel disconnected from our imagination and we will feel disconnected from society. We hope that people will come and visit us when we are ill and maybe they will bring us a ball of yarn and some knitting needles. My mom always spent hours coloring with my children when they were young, and she would say, "When I can no longer knit or sew, bring me a coloring book and crayons." My mother and father both keep their creativity high on their priority list, along with socializing.

So, what do we do? Every day and all daylong keep calling your energy back. Ask yourself , "What am I doing?" "I don't care what that person thinks or does." Call your energy back and remind yourself that you are not going to give that person or situation your currency.

Look yourself in the eyes and say a positive affirmation. "I have strong and supple toes and this will be a great day." "I have beautiful, thick, wavy hair and I love it." "Wow, that person must really be in a hurry and I wonder if they just saved me from a speeding ticket."

When you become aware of the decisions you make and your reactions, you will feel better and more in control of yourself. Soon you will bring those better feelings out into your household and your environment. You will feel happier about your life and relationships. By changing situations into less frustrating drama and turn it into a neutral thought or a positive affirmation, you are gaining your energy back. You will be able to symbolically call on your energy and bring yourself quickly to your center.

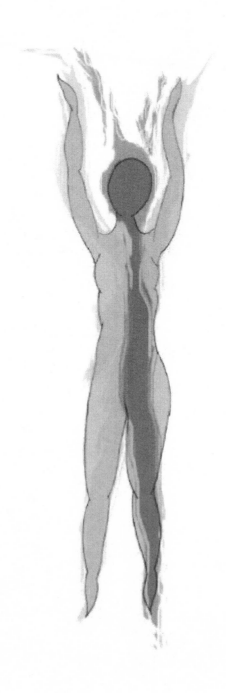

54

VISHNU - Altar

Sacred Space, Ritual

Vishnu is the omnipresent force that preserves the universe. With the act of creating an altar or sacred space we are connecting to that energy. Place items representing the five elements – Earth, Air, Water, Fire and Ether (Spirit) at the focal point of your sanctuary. Are you feeling lost? Do you feel fractured? Is there a craving of something else in your life? Rituals are acts that bring us back to our center, to our inner spirit and guidance. Light a candle, burn incense, bang a gong, smudge with sage, hum, chant, and say a blessing. All of these acts remind us that we are a part of greater consciousness. When you are feeling disjointed, lonely or empty, take the time to connect yourself through ritual. This is such a luxury to have time to do oracle cards, spin a pendulum, have a salts bath and light a candle. Come into your beautifully designed sacred space and embrace ritual while setting an intention.

How to do it: Place meaningful items on the altar. While lighting candles speak an intention either out loud or in your mind, "Spirit, allow me to hear your guidance." When smudging, light a bundle of sage, smoke each of the four corners as you repeat your intention. While practicing with a pendulum ask a question, and then notice if it spins in a circle "yes", or goes in a straight line "no.

I love to create an altar or many spaces in my home and in my office, which bring me back to my core or sushumna. I find it important to surround myself with beautiful items that inspire me to be the best person that I can be. Therefore, create an altar or sacred space. Vishnu is the omnipresent force, which reminds us that we are spiritual beings living here in the physical world. My altar reminds me to come back to eternal Goddess energy and acts as a reminder to connect to spirit for guidance and answers on how to be in service to others and to make a difference. It prompts me to continue to take steps in my own dharma (life purpose).

I create an altar with only items that represent good prana or energy in them. If the memory that they bring up isn't as pleasant as I would like it to be, I remove them. Take a look around the space you are in now, do you have in your possession anything, that when you look at it, you immediately think of something unpleasant? Perhaps it's something your husband received in a past relationship. Maybe you have an item that was passed on to you from a relative that you didn't care for, or a painting that triggers an unpleasant remembrance. Those are items that hold negative prana. If at all possible get rid of that memorabilia. Give them to charity or another family member who wants them. Change the energy of an item by burying it in salt and bathing it under the full moon.

I used to own a vase and every time I used it, I remembered a friendship with someone which ended in drama and sadness. One day it was full of flowers on my table and I thought, "Why do I still have that vase?" Yes, I liked the vase and it fit in with my décor, but I always felt sad when I thought of how our relationship ended. I got up that instant and changed the vase, later giving it away, knowing that not all sacred contracts end in joy.

Bring in treasures from nature; pieces collected on travels or items received from loved ones. I don't like a lot of clutter so I make the objects count, moving them around often to continue to see them. Have you ever noticed when we keep furnishings or accessories the same in our home for days, week and months, we stop seeing them? Even when we drive past buildings and landscapes over and over again our mind stops registering them. Therefore, it's beneficial to keep it fresh by moving and changing your alter each month.

On the evening of the full moon gently wash possessions with scented water. Recharge gems to gain the moons energy in them by placing them in various windows. As we change altars, they will reflect our own changes and growth, providing us an opportunity to honor life's cycles and connect to the femininity of the moon.

On the new moon meditate and write out desires of wishful manifestation. Then sleep with the intentions under your pillow every night until the full moon. On the full moon take time to re-address the wish list, recognizing what has manifested and whether you still have the same desires and aspirations.

On my altar I honor the five elements along with their corresponding cardinal directions: Air - North, Earth - East, Water - South, Fire - West, and Ether which is space or Spirit, so in my case Yogini or Goddess – Center. When I am doing divination I will make sure all the elements are in their corresponding directions, but while creating an altar on a table or dresser, place each item so they are esthetically pleasing.

Creating sacred space every month keeps it fresh and brings us back into our self and our important beautiful core essence. This ritual grounds us, and gives us an opportunity to re-connect by blessing our emotional realm, our physical warrior realm with our heart center.

ELEMENTS

- **Air** – North.
  Place an item in the Northern point to represent the element of **Air**. To symbolize air use a feather, burn incense or I own a small statue of a female holding a bird. The feather became the symbol of this book, so now I have a lot of feathers in my possession, which hold fantastic prana for me. Place the item

down connecting to what it represents. For air connect to the aspects of communication, relationships and choices. Ask yourself: How am I communicating these days and is there a conversation I need to have? Is there a book I want to read or some course I want to take? Have I been allowing core beliefs from stopping me? Have I shown up authentic in my relationships? This is an opportunity to check in, to take note and to put some energy into the air element.

- **Earth** – East.
  For the element of **Earth** place a rock, crystal, stick, leaf, flower or a plant on the altar. This item represents the earth and connection to getting things done, creating abundance and being stable. Have I been procrastinating? Is there something that I am doing that I don't like? What practical things can I switch up that will serve my higher good? Do I need to eat better, slower? Get more sleep? Catch up on my banking, or get bills paid? Remind yourself to strategically connect with the earth element. When earthly tasks get caught up and completed, feel a sense of accomplishment and pride.

- **Water** – South.
  For the element of **Water** I often use a shell found on my travels. A bowl can be used as a representation of water since it is a vessel to hold fluid. When I do divination I pour a goblet of water or wine to place on the altar. A mirror, image of a beach scene, or a container of sand can also be used. As you place your water item on your altar tap into the properties of movement, creativity, sexuality, sensuality and emotion. Ask yourself, am I living with creativity, music, dance, beauty and joy? Am I happy? What's been coming to me in meditation? What insights have I gained? When connecting to the water element we are given a chance to reflect on longings and feelings including reactions to emotions.

- **Fire** – West.
  For **Fire** it's easiest to light a candle. An image of a sunset, or fire can also be used. When lighting the candle or placing your fire item onto the altar, tap into your internal fire, your ego and

how you show up in the world. When outside and especially during divination, light a small fire. Create a ritual by writing a message on a paper of either what you want to attract or let go of and burn. Is this the time for me to turn it up and generate more? Are there some challenges I would like to step into? During this wonderful opportunity to connect to the fire element, notice fear that may be hovering around what you want to do next. We don't need to do anything with fear other than notice it.

- **Ether** - Goddess/God - Center.
  When I went to India I brought back several figurines of **Goddesses**, also I have beautiful statues of women in various yoga poses, or sometimes I'll use a painting or drawn image that represents **Yogini** to me. I ceremoniously place this sacred piece into the center of my alter. This small act gives an opportunity to honor the **Goddess** that resides within each of us. Let's remember our beautiful pure light, our soul that resides in our physical bodies. Feel your connection to spirit along with your guides and angels. Ask for what you need and call upon the divine to show you the signs to help you lead the way. Re-align to your divine feminine Shakti energy and value your feminine strength and essential offerings.

By creating sacred spaces, connecting monthly to the Divine and surrounding ourselves with items that are saturated in loving energy, we feed and nourish our soul. Designing an altar gives us daily reminders to come back to our authentic selves, who we really are and what we want to be in this lifetime. These rituals are pleasing and allow our feminine expression to radiate.

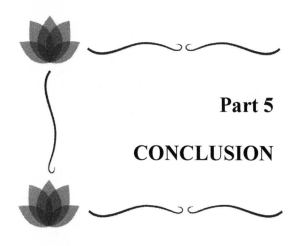

Part 5

CONCLUSION

Conclusion

We are all connected, and you matter to a world that needs you, the universe is ready for you and your offerings. Love who you are and decide the kind of life you will form. Be blessed and honored to know that you are an important and an integral part of creation. Show up with honesty and integrity and live without fear so your light will shine brightly into every corner of your existence. Shine your light, stand strong in your beauty, believe fully in yourself and own your greatness, your unique qualities that no one else has. Live your life fiercely and know that you can generate it into complete perfection. Know that you are loved and blessed.

What is it that you want to create for your life? How do you want to show up in this world and what do you want to leave behind? Find the tools and courage to embrace all the beauty and graceful flowing light that resides in you. Walk confidently through this earth and swim freely in our oceans and lakes. Stand fiercely in your formidable fire and blow breezes with an open and loving heart. Generously offer your gifts and your love to encourage all women to do the same. You get to choose what you create. You have a choice to listen to your intuition. Please don't disregard the voice of your soul.

Intuition Is A Choice.

Guided Meditations

𝓗er Story Meditation

𝒴 oni Mudra: Bring your hands into Yoni Mudra by lacing your fingers together then bring the tips of your pointer fingers and thumbs together.

Yoni is a softer word for vagina, and has a more pleasing sound vibration. Take this time to connect to your own inner Goddess. The beautiful feminine part of you that has unwavering strength of character, the kitten, minx or tiger that resides within. Connect to the passionate self that loves beauty and splendor, who wants to be pampered and cherished.

Sit up tall and imagine running energy down connecting you with Mother Earth!

Exhale your breath out and drop down into the belly. Take three full breaths and with each exhalation drop deeper into your feminine wisdom. Begin by feeling your connection to the earth. With your belly soft feel the original joy and natural relaxation of your tummy. Relax into this inborn state with yoni onto the earth. Allow your abdomen to relax. You don't have to hold it tight and engaged; you are safe to allow it to soften.

Feel how your belly has been nourished by meals that have been lovingly prepared for it. You feed yourself with healthful bits of luxury. Recognize enjoyment when you make food that is full of color and presented in a beautiful way. The flavors of sweet, sour, salty, savory, spicy or bitter foods. Remember what a privilege and pleasure it is when we enjoy a meal with our friends and with other goddesses.

Take this opportunity now to connect energetically, on an energetic level, to all the other beautiful, inspiring and creative Yogini's and Goddesses in your life. Some of them you may know very well, perhaps since childhood. Some inspiring women in your life may be your mother, sister or your friends while some may be strangers to you. Connect also to the Goddesses of past. Goddesses from traditions and cultures such as, Hindu Goddesses, Tibetan,

306

Greek, Roman, Egyptian, Celtic, Aboriginal or Mayan Goddesses. For this moment, notice which Goddess may be coming to you and rest in the knowledge that we are all connected. Know we are all connected. Feel the inspiration.

You may be on your moon cycle (menstruating), perhaps you have passed through into wise-woman (menopause); you may be with child, or without your womb. Wherever you are in the feminine process, take this moment to honor where you are on this day. Honor your own creative power, your sexuality and sensuality. Honor the vulnerability to share intimacy with another.

Take a deep breath in as you chant three times, a mantra to honor your feminine, creative, abundant and sacred belly.

Om Shri Shriyaya Namaha

Translation Chant: Om Shri Shriyaya Namaha – We honor the creative power of the great mother, the creative feminine power within each of us.

Three-Part Breath Meditation

While sitting in a chair, sit up nice and tall. Have your feet on the floor or on a stool without locking your knees. You can also do this while lying on your back. Remember to keep breathing, as you don't want to hold your breath. Keep lengthening your breath, and breathe smooth inhalations and exhalations.

1. Begin by placing your hands onto your lower belly just above your pubic bone. Start by taking long, slow, smooth, steady breaths all the way down to the lower part of your belly. Breathe into your palms. Keep your focus on the breath as your lower belly expands out with each inhalation and comes in with each exhalation. You can even use your abdominal muscles to pull your lower belly into your back on exhalations. Repeat this for 5-7 breaths.

2. On your next exhalation bring your hands around your rib cage. Visualize filling up your rib cage as you breathe into the ribs. As you inhale expand your ribs out towards your elbows, and as you exhale draw your elbows back towards each other. Focus your mind on bringing the breath to your ribs, as well as into your back. If lying on the floor feel your back press into your mat.
    Do this for 5-7 breaths.

3. On an exhalation place your hands onto your chest, just below the collarbone. Guide the breath to this area, still keeping the breath long, slow and smooth. Fill your lungs and chest with air on your inhalation and then exhale it all out.
    Do this for 5-7 breaths

4. Now we want to bring it all together. Bring your hands down by your sides and take your long breath to first fill up your lower belly, then your ribs, and lastly your chest. Exhale from

your lower belly, ribs, and chest. Again, inhale into your lower belly, ribcage, and chest. Exhale from the lower belly, ribcage and chest.

Repeat 5-15 full three-part breaths.

Doing this exercise is extremely helpful to relax your central nervous system, release tension, stress and anxiety from your body and your mind. This breathing technique can also be useful if you're unable to sleep. Since it is a form of meditation, make sure that you keep bringing your focus and awareness back to the breath. Whenever your mind wanders, and it will, ALWAYS bring your mind, awareness, and focus back onto guiding your breath.

Connecting Chakra Energy Meditation

Sitting up nice and tall begin by taking a couple long slow breaths. Now imagine a string of energy is coming down from the base of your spine. Imagine that energy is running down your legs, through your feet and going down through your house. Imagine those strings of energy are breaking through the earth's crust all the way down into the center of the earth. Now visualize tying a large golden nugget at the end of the string of energy. The nugget is keeping you connected to the earth, yet it is allowing you to sway with your own natural rhythm.

Now imagine drawing your awareness up that string of energy, all the way up until it comes to your pelvic floor. Here you connect to your root chakra at the base of your spine. You are connecting to your tribe, your family and the foundation of who you are. Connect to the abundance you have in your life and the life that you have on this earth. As you move your awareness, imagine moving up the string of energy to your sacral chakra of passion, emotions, sensuality and feelings in the water of the second chakra.

Moving your awareness up the string of energy towards your solar plexus where you connect to the fire element of your third chakra as power, ego, strength and how you show up. From here move your awareness up the string of energy to your heart chakra and air element of love, compassion and forgiveness. Next bring your awareness to your throat chakra of sound, authenticity and choices. Here's where you live with the ability to speak your truth.

From our throat we move our awareness to our third eye of intuition, how to walk on our path, dreaming and recognizing our soul. Bring your awareness now to the top of your head and your crown chakra. Imagine the string of energy rising up through and above the top of your head. Imagine the string is going up through the ceiling and the roof of your home. Imagine the string of energy continues to rise all the way up to the heavens. You can even imagine your Angels are grasping hold of the end of your string to keep you connected to the Divine.

Now imagine bringing your awareness back down the string of energy. All the way down into your body. Visualize energy running smoothly up and down the length of your body. Picture the string of energy is starting to increase so it is now the size of a straw. See the string growing to the size of a cylinder. The cylinder of energy is growing and expanding so that it is coming to the edges of your body. Fill it now with a beautiful, healing, loving and joyous white light and visualize extending it out through your body. Imagine the energy is expanding out the front, the sides and even the back of your body.

Feel the energy spread out two inches around your whole body, now extend it a little farther. Keep expanding your energy as far as you can and hold it there. See now if you can extend your energy just a little bit further. Move your energy as far out as you can. How does it feel? Gently and slowly draw your energy back in until it feels most comfortable for you. Stay with the sensations.

When you are ready, slowly open your eyes.

Isn't it wonderful to recognize how you can have control of your energy? That you have the ability to get yourself grounded, to tap into your sensuality, your power, compassion, choices, intuition and easily connect to your higher power. You can expand your energy out or you can draw your energy in. You can fill it with loving healing energy or not. You now know that you have the ability to heal.

Acknowledgments

$\mathcal{F}$irst I want to acknowledge and thank my fun, kind and realistic husband Daren. I love you and the life that we have created together. You have supported me, not only for all the time and energy put into this book and cards, but also for the many projects that I have stepped into over the years. I am so filled with gratitude for your love, encouragement, ability to make me laugh and acceptance.

My incredible and inspiring children Forrester, Chloe and Jenkins. I am enthralled at the amazing people that you are as you continue to inspire me as my greatest teachers. I live for our daily chats, love hearing your laughter and I admire all of your strengths of character. Each of you have stepped into life with purpose and resolution. I am so incredibly proud of you, knowing that you are here for greatness. Thank you for choosing me to be your Mom.

My parents, Joyce and Garth, I appreciate all the encouragement, awareness and wisdom over the years. You have remained examples of how to live with great love and passion for life that creates overall wellness and joy.

My sister Vicky, I am grateful for your continued support, offering your talent, insight and your ability to understand me with very few words. Your generosity is unparalleled to anyone else I have ever known and shows up as unconditional love. Thank you!

Thank you to all of my friends as well as my Diva sisters Dale, Dolly, Geri, Heather, Lisa and Pam. Recognizing the importance of having friends to laugh with, cry with, for support and encouragement. I love you for teaching me the power, meaning and importance of how to be a friend.

Karen Peterson Sainas, I am so thankful to the Divine for bringing us together and I am thrilled with our continued connection with each other. It is an exciting time as we embark in collaboration and staying true to our self-care practice as we show up on our quest to honor the significance of the Feminine.

Thank you so much Kerri Kelly. You embody the fierce, energetic and motivating force that has consistently coached and encouraged me through this entire process and more. You have a way of knowing what a person needs to hear and a way of saying it that ignites action.

313

Teachers and Mentors

*D*ali Lama I heard speak at the Calgary Saddledome Stadium on September 29, 2009, which was thought provoking and encouraging.

Integrative Yoga Therapy Instructors: Serena Arora and Sandra Coombe. My initial Yoga Teacher Instructors who got me started on this Yogic path and helped me recognize that this is my calling.

Off the Mat, Into the World™ founders Seane Corn, Hala Khouri and Suzanne Sterling have been hugely instrumental in me becoming the person I am today. I owe them an enormous debt of gratitude for their teaching, encouragement and opportunity to show up and step into a leadership role. If it were not for them I would not have been given such strong examples and skills.

Global Seva Challenge, India provided the life changing experience of raising $20,000.00 and then traveling to India. Thank you Dream Team: Chelsey, Chloe, Daisy, Denise, Elisa, Jayne, Linda, Rhona and Val.

Anodea Judith, Goddess of the Chakras is an inspiration and a light, as well as a groundbreaking Spiritual Leader in her field. Anodea Judith's work inspired my love of the chakra system. Attending training with her, she showed me how to remain humble and authentic.

Pandit Rajmani Tiqunait of the Himalayan Institute, thank you for the teachings and experiences I gained on the Kumbha Mela pilgrimage which have been astronomical.

Caroline Myss' books and webinars have without fail helped me get clear on my own teachings and to continue to move forward into transformation.

Louise Hay *Heal Your Body and You Can Heal Your Life* by Louise L Hay and published through Hay House are both excellent books. Louise's work with affirmations is an integral part of my life and my work. Affirmations are necessary for us all to use on a daily basis.

I also want to thank and acknowledge Angela Ditch for all of your insight as well as connecting me with Tom Bird.

Tom Bird Writing Retreat and Sojourn Publishing, LLC was a brilliant method for getting my book out. I'd like to offer a special acknowledgement to Rama Jon Coogan who helped make this process smooth and relatively easy.

About the Author

*C*andace McKim Author of *Yogini's Guide - Intuition Is A Choice* and *Yogini's Guide to Intuition* Oracle Cards.

Candace lives in Alberta, Canada on an acreage with her loving husband, Daren and aging dog, Coal. Her three children, Forrester, Chloe and Jenkins are all off living full lives. As newly empty nesters, Candace and Daren enjoy time in nature kayaking, hiking, skiing and camping as well as travelling and celebrating with good friends and family.

Candace's life work is in support of The Woman who is trying to be everything to everyone, hoping her life looks beautifully perfect. On the inside this Woman feels something is missing, she yearns for connection. As she hears the voice of her intuition she fears stepping wholly into her purpose and femininity, afraid of ridicule, confrontation and loss of security.

Through interactive workshops, inspirational talks, personal counseling, retreats and her book; Candace guides you to identify your path, supporting you to courageously stay connected to your intuition and value your femininity.

Book, Oracle Cards, Yoga Videos and Meditations are available on Candace's website www.candacemckim.com

Photo's of Candace McKim ©2014 Heide Van Loon Photography

About the Artist

*C*hloe McKim is an art student completing her Fine Arts Degree with plans to go on to get her Masters. Perhaps in Berlin.

Chloe is currently enrolled at Alberta College of Art + Design and majoring in ceramics. In her early years, Chloe explored a love for both fibre and jewelry design before realizing that ceramics is her true passion. She has completed a semester abroad in Bergen, Norway, and attended the Bergen Academy of Art and Design. In studies abroad, she was able to bolster a large range of new and unique techniques that have inspired her ever-growing practice. Chloe's current work consists of sculpting still life; she is able to see the beauty in capturing the permanence of memories and past. Drawn to design with a monochromatic palette, she takes joy in revealing small details or hidden treasures.

Beneath this orchestra of immense talent, Chloe is a calm and selfless person and her mantra flows through each drawing scribed on the pages of this book. When asked to present the art by mother and author Candace McKim, Chloe jumped at the opportunity to showcase her undeniable gift.

Made in the USA
Charleston, SC
10 August 2015